So, You Think You Know Cape Cod?

People, Places, Folklore, Trivia and Treasures

By Henry M. Quinlan
Photos by Emily E. Murphy

Omni Publishing Co.
2022

Copyright @ 2022

By Henry M. Quinlan

All rights reserved,
Including the right of reproduction
In whole or in part in any form.

Published by Omni Publishing Co.
www.omni-pub.com

Photography: Emily E. Murphy

Cover Design: Dave Derby
www.DerbyCreative.com

Library of Congress cataloging in publication data
Quinlan, Henry
So, You Think You Know Cape Cod?
People, Places, Folklore, Trivia and Treasures

ISBN: 978-1-928758-04-4

Preface

I have been traveling to Cape Cod for more than 70 years, and I still get a good feeling when I first spot the bridge, either one - the Sagamore or the Bourne. As I go over either bridge, I think of what lies below them. One of the finest walking places anywhere. The walk along the Canal, on either side, is to be enjoyed as you watch a variety of boats travel by, and you pass fishermen casting their lines from their spots hoping to catch "the big one."

Going over the Sagamore Bridge, Route 6 is the fastest option to any destination on the Cape. But you also can drop down and ride along the meandering Route 6A. This is the entry to what many call the "old Cape Cod." The road is lined with buildings and places that speak of the Cape's history. From the stately mansions of the old sea captains to the white churches to the cemeteries, they provide a record of that history. If you have the time - and the ride will encourage you to take the time - read the plaques on the buildings and the historic markers, which tell you the history of Cape Cod. Route 6A extends to Provincetown but vanishes within US Route 6 in Eastham, Wellfleet and South Truro. Route 6A re-emerges in North Truro at Shore Road and extends to Provincetown, ending at the US Route 6 junction at Herring Cove.

The traveler who wishes a quicker route, following Route 6 will take you to your destination much faster than Route 6A. It goes up the middle of Cape Cod with many of its arteries leading to the beautiful beaches and oceanside towns where the Cape's reputation as wonderful vacation spot was created.

If you go over the Bourne Bridge, you are on your way to the Upper Cape and the beach communities of Bourne, Falmouth, and Mashpee. Barnstable, the commercial hub of Cape Cod, can be accessed over either bridge and is home to some of the finest beaches on Cape Cod.

Cape Cod has provided lifetime memories for millions of visitors, and I include myself in that group. I hope this book will reveal to the reader some treasures of Cape Cod they have not discovered.

Author Information

Henry M. Quinlan – *Grandfather*

Henry M. Quinlan, a graduate of Boston College and Suffolk University Law School, is a resident of Mattapoisett, MA. He has been in the publishing business for more than 50 years and is currently the owner and publisher of Omni Publishing Co.

His proudest accomplishment in publishing was publishing the book *Make Way for Ducklings* in Moscow in Russian at the request of President G. H. W. Bush in 1991 as part of the 1992 Summit between Presidents Bush and Gorbachev, and to arrange the erection of the *Make Way for Ducklings* statues in Moscow.

He currently gives talks about his experiences in Russia, about building your Emotional Pension and how to write and self-publish "Your Story." He has assisted many senior citizens in writing and self-publishing, notably three men between the age of 88 and 90 years old. (www.hmqpublisher.com)

This is the second book in a series. The first book was "So, You Think You Know the South Coast?"

Emily E. Murphy – *Granddaughter*

Emily E. Murphy is a resident of Mattapoisett, MA, and a 2022 graduate of Old Rochester Regional High School. She is a four-year member of the Girls Tennis Team and 2022 Captain. She will enroll as a freshman at Providence College in the fall.

Publisher: Omni Publishing Co. www.omni-pub.com

Table of Contents

Cape Cod 7

Barnstable 9

Bourne 21

Brewster 27

Chatham 33

Dennis 43

Eastham 49

Falmouth 55

Harwich 67

Mashpee 73

Orleans 81

Provincetown 87

Sandwich 97

Truro 105

Wellfleet 111

Yarmouth 115

Treasures of Cape Cod 123

Cape Cod Indigenous People - The Wampanoag Tribe 135

Women of Cape Cod 139

Trivia 143

Photos 151

"Cape Cod baseball dates back to the time of the Civil War. A poster at the Hall of Fame in Cooperstown touts a round-trip train ride from Hyannis to Sandwich on July 4, 1885 - the occasion of the 14th annual baseball game between Sandwich and Barnstable."

Author: Jane Leavy

Cape Cod

On 15 May 1602, having made landfall from the west and believing it to be an island, Bartholomew Gosnold initially named this area "Shoal Hope." Later that day, after catching a "great store of codfish," he chose instead to name this outermost tip of land "Cape Cod." Notably, that name referred specifically to the area of modern-day Provincetown; it wasn't until much later that that name was reused to designate the entire region now known as Cape Cod. On 9 November 1620, the Pilgrims aboard the Mayflower sighted Cape Cod while en route to the Colony of Virginia.

After two days of failed attempts to sail south against the strong winter seas, they returned to the safety of the harbor, known today as Provincetown Harbor, and set anchor. It was here that the Mayflower Compact was drawn up and signed. They agreed to settle and build a self-governing community and came ashore in the West End. As defined by the Cape Cod Commission's enabling legislation, Cape Cod is conterminous with Barnstable County, Massachusetts. It extends from Provincetown in the northeast to Woods Hole in the southwest and is bordered by Plymouth to the northwest. The Cape is divided into fifteen towns, several of which are in turn made up of multiple named villages. Cape Cod forms the southern boundary of the Gulf of Maine, which extends north-eastward to Nova Scotia. Since 1914, most of Cape Cod has been separated from the mainland by the Cape Cod Canal. The canal cuts 7 miles roughly across the base of the peninsula, though small portions of the Cape Cod towns of Bourne and Sandwich lie on the mainland side of the canal. Two highway bridges cross the Cape Cod Canal: the Sagamore Bridge and the Bourne Bridge. In addition, the Cape Cod Canal Railroad Bridge carries railway freight and provides limited passenger service onto the Cape.

Cape Cod is a popular retirement area; 27.8% of the population of Barnstable County is 65 years old or older, and the average age of residents is the highest of any area in New England. Cape Cod is majority

Democrat, but by a smaller margin than the rest of Massachusetts. The bulk of the land in the area is glacial terminal moraine and represents the southernmost extent of glacial coverage in southeast New England; similar glacial formations make up Long Island in New York and Block Island in Rhode Island.

Image of Cape Cod from space.

> "The time must come when this coast (Cape Cod) will be a place of resort for those New-Englanders who really wish to visit the sea-side. At present it is wholly unknown to the fashionable world, and probably it will never be agreeable to them. If it is merely a ten-pin alley, or a circular railway, or an ocean of mint-julep, that the visitor is in search of, — if he thinks more of the wine than the brine, as I suspect some do at Newport, — I trust that for a long time he will be disappointed here. But this shore will never be more attractive than it is now."
>
> Author: Henry David Thoreau, *Cape Cod*

All About Barnstable

The Town of Barnstable (/ˈbɑːrnstəbəl/ BARN-stə-bəl) is a town in the state of Massachusetts and the county seat of Barnstable County. Barnstable is the largest community, both in land area and population, on Cape Cod, and is one of thirteen Massachusetts municipalities that have been granted city forms of government by the Commonwealth of Massachusetts but wish to retain "the town of" in their official names. At the 2020 census it had a population of 48,916. The town contains several villages (one of which is also named Barnstable) within its boundaries. Its largest village, Hyannis, is the central business district of the county and home to Barnstable Municipal Airport, the airline hub of Cape Cod and the islands of Martha's Vineyard and Nantucket. Additionally, Barnstable is a 2007 winner of the All-America City Award.

Barnstable takes its name from the English town of Barnstaple, in the county of Devon. The first European to explore the area was Bartholomew Gosnold in 1602. It was settled in 1638, as one of the first towns in the Plymouth Colony, one year behind Sandwich further south in Massachusetts on Cape Cod. It was incorporated on September 4, 1639, the same day as the towns of Sandwich, and Yarmouth. On the first Tuesday of December, the same year, its deputies took their seats in the general court. The early settlers were farmers, led by the Reverend Joseph Hull, the founder of Barnstable. A memorial tablet was dedicated there in 1939 (the 300th anniversary of the town's founding) marking the site of his home, and the rock from which he preached still stands along the highway there.

Soon after the town's founding, agriculture, fishing and salt works became its major industries. By the end of the 19th century, there were some 804 ships harbored in the town. But the role of sailing ships declined with the rise of ocean-going steamships and the railroad, which had arrived in 1854.

By the late 19th century, Barnstable was becoming world-renowned as the tourist destination it still is to this day. Many prominent Bostonians spent their summers on the Cape shores, as did presidents Ulysses S. Grant and Grover Cleveland. The most well-known family of the 20th century to summer in the town was, and remains, the Kennedy family.

In 1928 Rose and Joseph P. Kennedy, Sr. purchased a six acre house and property in Hyannis Port. President Kennedy and his brother, Robert, later purchased nearby homes. The Kennedy family still inhabit the Kennedy Compound in Hyannis Port. This was the summer home of President John F. Kennedy during his administration, and it was likewise the home of Senator Ted Kennedy until his death.

Today, tourists come in droves to the town during the summer months. Hyannis has numerous shops. Other attractions include the John F. Kennedy Museum and several other museums. Significant sites and renowned historic houses listed on the National Register of Historic Places include the Ancient Burying Ground and Gideon Hawley House, representing the town's colonial history. The town's many beaches are popular tourist destinations as well.

The Town of Barnstable contains several villages, which are not legally defined entities. Between seven and eleven are commonly enumerated, listed below with ZIP codes:

> The village of Barnstable (02630), including Cummaquid (02637)
> Centerville (02632)
> Cotuit (02635)
> Hyannis (02601), including Hyannis Port (02647)
> and West Hyannisport (02672)
> Marstons Mills (02648)
> Osterville (02655)
> West Barnstable (02668)

To the north of Barnstable lie the dunes of Sandy Neck along Barnstable Harbor, tipped by the Sandy Neck Light. The central part of the town is dominated by the pines and oaks around Wequaquet Lake. The south is where the bulk of the population lives, many along the beaches of Centerville and Hyannis Harbors. Hyannis is the biggest village in Barnstable by size and population.

People of Significance – Barnstable

Rev. John Lothropp (1584–1653) — was an English Anglican clergyman, who became a Congregationalist minister and emigrant to New England. He was among the first settlers of Barnstable. Perhaps Lothropp's principal claim to fame is that he was a strong proponent of the idea of the Separation of Church and State (also called "Freedom of Religion"). This idea was considered heretical in England during his time, but eventually became the mainstream view of people in the United States of America, because of the efforts of John Lothropp and others. Lothropp left an indelible mark on the culture of New England, and through that, upon the rest of the country. He has had many notable descendants, including at least six US presidents, as well as many other prominent Governors, government leaders, leaders of the Church of Jesus Christ of Latter-day Saints, and business people.

There, within three years of moving to Barnstable in 1639, Lothropp and his followers had built homes for all the families and then Lothropp began construction on a larger, sturdier meeting house adjacent to Coggin's (or Cooper's) Pond, which was completed in 1644. This building, now part of the Sturgis Library in Barnstable, is one of John Lothrop's original homes and meeting houses, and is now also the oldest building housing a public library in the USA.

Among his descendants there are:
4 U.S. Presidents:
Ulysses S. Grant, Franklin D. Roosevelt, George H. W. Bush
George W. Bush
Early leaders of The Church of Jesus Christ of Latter-day Saints:
Joseph Smith, Hyrum Smith, Wilford Woodruff, Oliver Cowdery, Parley P. Pratt, Orson Pratt
State governors:
Jeb Bush, Thomas E. Dewey, Jon Huntsman, Jr.,
William W. Kitchin, Sarah Palin, George W. Romney,
Mitt Romney, Jim Guy Tucker

James Otis Jr. (February 5, 1725 – May 23, 1783) was an American lawyer, political activist, pamphleteer, and legislator in Boston, a member of the Massachusetts provincial assembly, and an early advocate of the Patriot views against the policy of Parliament which led to the American Revolution. His well-known catchphrase "Taxation without Representation is tyranny" became the basic Patriot position. Otis was born in West Barnstable, the first of 13 children and the first to survive infancy.

Otis did not identify himself as a revolutionary; his peers, too, generally viewed him as more cautious than the incendiary Samuel Adams. Otis at times counseled against the mob violence of the radicals and argued against Adams's proposal for a convention of all the colonies resembling that of the Glorious Revolution of 1688. Yet, on other occasions, Otis exceeded Adams in rousing passions and exhorting people to action. He even called his compatriots to arms at a town meeting on September 12, 1768, according to some accounts

Austin Bearse (1808-1881) was a sea captain from Cape Cod who provided transportation for fugitive slaves in the years leading up to the American Civil War.

Bearse was born in Barnstable, on April 3, 1808. As a youth he worked occasionally as a mate on slave-trading vessels off the coast of South Carolina and saw firsthand how cruelly the slaves were treated. Decades later, he recalled in his memoir that "they were separated from their families and connections with as little concern as calves and pigs are selected out of a lot of domestic animals." Often the families and friends of the departing slaves were allowed to spend the night on the ship before it set sail. When morning came, Bearse had the unpleasant duty of warning them that it was time to say goodbye, and, as he put it, "the shrieks and cries of grief at these times were enough to make anyone's heart ache."

Affected by these experiences, Bearse became an abolitionist. He continued working as a seaman but refused to trade below the Mason-Dixon Line.

Thomas Hinckley (bapt. March 19, 1618 – April 25, 1706) was the last governor of the Plymouth Colony. Born in England, he came to North America as a teenager, and was a leading settler of what is now Barnstable. He served in a variety of political and military offices before becoming governor of the colony in 1680, a post he held (excluding the interregnum of the Dominion of New England 1686-1689) until the colony was folded into the Province of Massachusetts Bay in 1692. A monument, created in 1829 at the Lothrop Hill cemetery in Barnstable, attests to his "piety, usefulness and agency in the public transactions of his time."

Mercy Otis Warren was born on September 7, 1728, the third of thirteen children and first daughter of Colonel James Otis (1702–1778) and Mary Allyne Otis (1702–1774). The family lived in West Barnstable. Her mother was a descendant of Mayflower passenger Edward Doty.

In 1805, she completed her literary career with a three-volume History of the Rise, Progress, and Termination of the American Revolution. President Thomas Jefferson ordered subscriptions for himself and his cabinet and noted his "anticipation of her truthful account of the last thirty years that will furnish a more instructive lesson to mankind than any equal period known in history. The book's sharp comments on John Adams led to a heated correspondence and a breach in her friendship with Adams, which lasted until 1812.

John Percival (3 April 1779 – 7 September 1862), known as **Mad Jack Percival**, was a celebrated officer in the United States Navy during the Quasi-War with France, the War of 1812, the campaign against West Indies pirates, and the Mexican–American War.

John Adams - visited his college classmate, Johnathan Allen, at Chilmark Martha's Vineyard (1760); stayed at Newcomb Tavern in Sandwich en route to visit the American Patriot, James Otis Jr., in West Barnstable (1774).

Ulysses S. Grant - traveled on a special three-car train for the inauguration of the Old Colony Railroad, namesake of the Cape Cod Central Railroad, from Hyannis to Provincetown then ferried to Oak Bluffs Martha's Vineyard for a visit (1874).

Do You Know – Barnstable?

Kalmus Beach in Hyannis is named after Herbert Thomas Kalmus who played a major role in developing color motion picture film.

In 2012, the main house at the **Kennedy Compound** was donated to the Edward M. Kennedy Institute for the United States Senate.

The basement of the main house on the Kennedy Compound contains a motion-picture theater and a hall covered with dolls from all around the world. A wine cellar designed after a ship's hull and a sipping room – one of the Kennedy family's favorite hideouts.

In 1962, President John F. Kennedy and first lady Jacqueline Kennedy rented and converted the gray-shingled Morton Downey house on Squaw Island into a "summer White House" — when Secret Service became concerned about the proximity of the nearby Kennedy compound to its neighbors.

U.S. Secretary of the Interior Deb Haaland recently designated the word "squaw" a racial slur. She seeks to ban the word from federal lands. Haaland, the First American Indian appointed to a Cabinet post will create a task force that will evaluate 650 locations and rename them.

Osterville was originally named Cotacheset, based on the Native American name for the area. Over time it became a center for "oystering" (harvesting wild oysters) and was renamed Oysterville. Later a map misspelled the name as Osterville and the village became so.

In a quiet corner of Cape Cod called Osterville lies **Armstrong-Kelley Park**. Owned by the 76-year-old Cape Cod Horticultural Society. The 74-year young wonderland in the woods is Cape Cod's oldest (1930) and largest (8.5 acres) privately owned park open free to the public.

Located on Pine Street in Centerville Village is the **St. Francis Xavier cemetery**, which is the final resting place for Eunice Kennedy Shriver and her husband Sargent Shriver.

Alice Owen Williams, a retired teacher and trustee of Centerville Public Library established and operated the used book store at the library, which continues to provide additional funding to the library.

Old West Barnstable Cemetery (corner Rts. 149 and 6A) is the final resting place of hometown hero, **Captain John "Mad Jack" Percival**, who captained the USS Constitution (a/k/a "Old Ironsides") on her around-the-world journey from 1844-1846.

3365 Main St., Hyannis is the location of the **oldest wooden jail** in the United States, dating back to the late 1600s. Some say a few former inmates still haunt the building today.

Barnstable is one of thirteen Massachusetts municipalities that have applied for, and been granted, city forms of government but wish to retain "the town of" in their official names.

The **Ancient Burying Ground (or Phinney's Lane Cemetery)** is a historical cemetery at Phinney's Lane in Barnstable. It is the oldest cemetery in the village of Centerville, and the only surviving civic element of its colonial origins. It was listed on the National Register of Historic Places in 1987. The oldest marked grave in the cemetery is that of Jonathan Hamblen in 1743.

On July 4, 1980, two small business owners made their dream of making crunchy, delicious, unique quality potato chips a reality. They set up a small storefront in Hyannis where their chips quickly became a local favorite. Now they are available around the world. The **Cape Cod Potato Chips** factory is open to the public.

Every year the Cape's largest cultural event takes place in Hyannis Village Green. It is the annual **Pops by the Sea** concert by the Boston Pops Esplanade Orchestra led by Keith Lockhart. It is a fundraising event for the Arts Foundation of Cape Cod.

One of the Barnstable's hidden gems is **Kalmus Beach**, a 5 - minute bike ride from downtown Hyannis. It has powdery white sand and crystal-clear waters. It's surrounding by water on three sides, which makes it ideal for windsurfing and waterspouts. There is a parking lot or if you wish to walk, it is just up from Veteran's Park Beach.

If you are looking for quality ice cream there is a shop on Main Street in Centerville that is waiting for you, **Four Seas Ice Cream**, established in 1934, and features home-made ice cream. It has been ranked as one of the best in the country.

The Osterville Historical Museum, established in 1931, preserves the history of Osterville for all of those who love her, past, present, and future. The museum includes the largest collection of **wooden boats** in Massachusetts and is home to the Crosby Boats. The Crosbys are America's oldest, currently active, wooden boat building family.

This comment on the **Luke's Love Boundless Playground** website says it best.

"Great for the smaller set. Epic place for up to 8-10 yo. Rubberized ground equipment and clean. Challenging stuff for the bolder kids and low-level fun for the more cautious ones. Take your tots here to burn energy. God Bless the ones who built this."

It is in West Barnstable on Rte 149.

The **Olde County Courthouse in West Barnstable** was the site of a mass protest on Sept. 27, 1774, after Britain abrogated Massachusetts Bay's 1691 charter — one of a series of Coercive Acts intended to punish the colonists for the Boston Tea Party the previous year. As a result of the protest, all Barnstable County officials agreed to ignore Parliament's new rules, effectively freeing Cape Cod of British control.

In West Barnstable is the six-mile-long **Sandy Neck Barrier Beach** which protects the extensive Great Marshes, the latter a source of salt hay that attracted the first English settlers to the area in the mid-17th century.

The Cotuit Oyster Company dates to 1837 and is still cultivating the distinctive Cotuit Oysters with their unique flavor, producing the oldest brand name of oysters in the United States. Cotuit is world-famous for its oysters, and in years past they rivaled Wellfleet oysters and could be found on menus in restaurants from San Francisco to Paris.

Cotuit Skiffs, formerly known as Cotuit Mosquitos, are 14-foot gaff-rigged "one-design" sailboats that have been sailed on the waters of Cotuit Bay for the last 104 years, making them one of the oldest continuously sailed fleets of one-design racing boats in the world.

They were designed by Stanley Butler after the turn of the 20th century and were modeled after the flat-bottomed skiffs used in the oyster and commercial clam trade. Those boats were built with hard chines and low gunwales to provide a stable platform from which to calm from. The design was altered many times until 1926 when the design was standardized.

Marstons Mills has many notable lakes, cranberry bogs, and ponds, including Mystic Lake, Middle Pond, Hamblin Pond, and Shubael Pond. Marstons Mills has no saltwater beaches. Although Prince Cove has salt water access, it does not have a public beach, only a town-owned marina and boat ramp.

Isaiah Thomas Books and Prints is a general used and rare book shop, strong in many fields, including art, architecture, and photography, first edition, and miniature books. It is located in the Village of Cotuit and has have approximately 70,000 books in all fields.

Sturgis library building: the house which forms the original part of the library is the oldest building housing a public library in the United States. The building is also one of the oldest houses remaining on Cape Cod. Since Reverend Lothrop used the front room of the house for public worship, another distinction of the Sturgis Library is that it is the oldest structure still standing in America where religious services were regularly held. This room, now called "The Lothrop Room," has two distinctions with its beamed ceiling and pumpkin-colored wide-board floors, retains the quintessential early character of authentic Cape Cod houses.

In 2017 *House Beautiful* magazine listed Barnstable one of the **happiest towns in the nation** and the town of Barnstable on Cape Cod. In addition, a nationwide Gallup study named Barnstable Town the second-happiest place in America in terms of depression rates and wellbeing.

The reason the home of the **Barnstable Comedy Club** is still known as the Village Hall is because in 1961 when the club purchased the Hall from the Barnstable Women's Club there was a condition in the sale agreement that the name of the building remain, the Village Hall. The Barnstable Comedy Club is located at 3171 Main Street, Barnstable.

The **Coast Guard Heritage Museum** that sits at the corner of Main Street and Millway in Barnstable Village is one of only two free standing museums celebrating the Coast Guard history in the country. The building was built in 1856 as the U.S. Customs House in Barnstable.

Barnstable's Old Jail built in the 1600s is one of the oldest in America. The jail could hold about six prisoners. One notable detainee was Goody Hallett, who was imprisoned in 1716. Hallett was known as the Witch of Wellfleet and was the lover of famed pirate Samuel Bellamy. It is Located at 3353 Main St, Barnstable.

The **Sandy Neck Nature Trail** is one of the easiest and most spectacular walking trails on Cape Cod. Its length is 7.4 miles and at its highest point is only 54 inches above sea level.

Books by the Sea, in Centerville, is the perfect place to find a great book to read, whether it is for the beach or at home, in a very calming atmosphere. The staff has all the knowledge about the latest best sellers as well as the classic Cape Cod read. Don't forget to visit the used book section past best sellers.

Cattle and the harvesting of salt marsh hay was the primary economic activity in colonial Cotuit. **The Little River** section of the village (near the present location of the Cotuit Oyster Company) was the site of some early shipyards.

Isaiah Thomas Books and Prints is a general used and rare book shop, strong in many fields, including art, architecture, and photography, first edition, and miniature books. It is located in the Village of Cotuit and has approximately 70,000 books in all fields.

Sampsons Island is a 15-acre uninhabited, undeveloped barrier island at the mouth of Cotuit Harbor in Barnstable. It is the location of the Massachusetts Audubon Society's **Sampsons Island Wildlife Sanctuary**, and it forms part of the Sampsons Island/Dead Neck Island barrier beach system. The island is only accessible by private boat and is used for recreation and wildlife viewing and preservation.

The name **Cotuit** is derived from the Wampanoag term: "place of the council." Cotuit was formerly known as Cotuit Port until the postmaster, Charles C. Bearse, dropped the "port" in 1872.

Bread + Roses Bookshop features "good reads, good eats, good folks, good trouble." It was designed to nourish your body, enrich your mind and to celebrate your soul. Politically engaged, and artist and queer friendly, it also features a plant-based café.

The Oyster Harbors Club was established in 1926 and features an 18-hole championship course designed by Donald Ross as well as John and Frederick Olmstead. The course was updated and restored to its original design in 2009 by Tom Doak of Renaissance Golf Design.

The landscape on **Oyster Harbors** had been done by the Olmsted Brothers, top landscape architects of their time, who had also designed Central Park in New York, and the golf course was designed by prominent golf course architect, Donald Ross.

Between 1925 and 1967 **Oyster Harbors Club** was owned by investors and stockholders, which for many years members did not know. At that time there was no initiation fee to be a member (members were invite only) and annual dues were paid on April first. If one had not received a bill for their annual dues, one would understand that he was no longer a member and could no longer use the facilities. These conditions existed until the establishment of the new club in 1968.

Located on Pine Street, Centerville is the **St. Francis Xavier Cemetery**, which is the final resting place for Eunice Kennedy Shriver and her husband Sargent Shriver.

Craigville Beach is located on Nantucket Sound. It is located in Craigville (part of Centerville) and is a very popular tourist hot spot on Cape Cod. Unlike many private Cape beaches which offer parking to residents only, Craigville is a public beach area, available to non-residents for a daily parking fee. In the summer, kite surfing is extremely popular.

Craigville beach consists of two separate beaches. The public beach, **Craigville Beach** and the resident beach, **Covell's Beach**.

The statue of John F. Kennedy walking barefoot through the sand and grass of Cape Cod was designed by noted sculptor David Lewis and stands in front of the JFK museum in downtown Hyannis.

All About Bourne

Bourne was first settled in 1640 by Ezra Perry as a part of the town of Sandwich. Prior to its separation from Sandwich, the area was referred to as West Sandwich. The townspeople incorporated Bourne in 1884, the last town to be incorporated in Barnstable County and named it for Jonathan Bourne Sr. (1811–1889), whose ancestor Richard Bourne represented Sandwich in the first Massachusetts General Court and was the first preacher to the Mashpee Wampanoag on Cape Cod. The town lies at the northeast corner of Buzzards Bay and is the site of Aptucxet Trading Post, the nation's oldest store.

It was founded by the Pilgrims in 1627 at a site halfway between the two rivers which divided Cape Cod from the rest of the state. It was out of this location that the Cape Cod Canal was formed, in order to save time and lives by eliminating the need to sail around the hazardous eastern shores of the Cape. Because of the canal, Bourne is now considered the "first" town on the Cape, as all three bridges (the Bourne, Sagamore and the Cape Cod Canal Railroad Bridge) are located within the town. Its 10 village are: Bourne Village, Bournedale, Buzzards Bay, Cataumet, Gray Gables, Monument Beach, Otis Air Base, Pocasset, Sagamore, and Sagamore Beach.

Most of Bourne is on Cape Cod, but Buzzards Bay and Sagamore Beach are on the mainland side with Buttermilk Bay forming the western edge of the peninsula.

Bourne is the site of the Massachusetts Maritime Academy, a maritime college located at the southern mouth of the canal on the western shore. Otis Air National Guard Base is partially located in the town. The Air Force Space Command system PAVE PAWS northeast radar is located within the base.

Bourne is home to an archaeological curiosity known as the "Bourne stone," featuring markings whose origin and significance have not been conclusively established.

People of Significance – Bourne

Jonathan Bourne (1811–1889) was a New Bedford alderman, major investor in the whaling business, member of executive councils of Massachusetts governors George D. Robinson and Oliver Ames, and namesake of the town of Bourne.

Jonathan was one of ten children and at the age of 17 left home for New Bedford. He prospered and became the town's most successful owner of whaling ships. In 1884 he was a state legislator, and when the western half of Sandwich petitioned the Commonwealth for separation as a town, he was helpful on their behalf. The leaders showed their appreciation by naming the new town in his honor. Thus in 1884 the newest town on Cape Cod came from the oldest town, Sandwich. Jonathan's ancestor was the **Rev. Richard Bourne**, the first preacher to the Indians.

With the signing of the first private commercial contract in English-speaking North America, Aptucxet became the first private commercial enterprise using a local currency known as wampum and launched what is now the world's leading economic force: the American Free Enterprise System.

Wampum is a polished fragment of a hard-shell clam usually containing a purple color and shaped in a cylindrical form. The local Native Americans called the clams quahogs (pronounced kwo-hogs), and making the wampum required a great amount of effort and skill.

The first archaeological dig on the property, Aptucxet, was conducted in 1852 when **John Batchelder** and **William Russell** undertook a partial excavation of a double cellar hole foundation. They believed that the foundation was part of the original Aptucxet Trading Post.

To stimulate interest, a historical exhibition was held, and donations were received, enabling the Society to purchase the lot of land on which two cellar holes were located, marking the site of the trade house. In 1926, **President Percival Lombard** and **Vice President Nathan**

Bourne Hartford uncovered the complete foundations and many interesting relics. Additional lots were purchased, bringing the total to about twelve acres. The structure existing today is a replica erected on the original foundation.

View along the Cape Cod Canal, where walkers and bicyclists enjoy views of the canal's various boat traffic, along with the area's quaint shoreline scenery of unique homes and natural beauty.

Do You Know – Bourne?

The **Jonathan Bourne Historical Center,** overlooking the Cape Cod Canal, was built in 1896 as the Town Library. A handsome stained-glass window depicting "St. Michael and the Dragon," by Clayton & Bell of London, England, graces the former reading room.

Bourne is also home of the **National Marine Life Center**, an independent, non-profit, rehabilitation and release hospital for the treatment of stranded sea turtles and seals. The goal of the Center is to become the primary care center and information hub on Cape Cod regarding marine animals and their environment.

Massachusetts Maritime Academy is in Buzzard's Bay, which is a part of Bourne. Massachusetts Maritime Academy is a public college established in 1891 and is the second oldest state maritime academy in the United States and ranked as the number one Massachusetts University for ROI (return on investment).

The Bourne Stone, a 300-pound chunk of granite upon which two lines of carvings were drawn, continues to be a mystery to historians. The origin of the carver or the meanings of the markings are unknown despite many attempts. The stone is on view in the museum rooms of the Bourne Historical Society in the Jonathan Bourne Historical Center, Bourne Village.

President Grover Cleveland owned a summer estate in Bourne Village, Gray Gables, that served as the Summer White House from 1893 to 1896. The building was destroyed in a fire in 1973.

The **Aptucxet Trading Post Museum** is a small open-air historical museum in Bourne. The main attraction is a replica of the 17th-century Aptucxet Trading Post which was built by the Pilgrims of Plymouth Colony in order to trade with the Wampanoag Indians and the Dutch. It was the first permanent community on Cape Cod. The property, listed on the National Register of Historic Places in 2021, also has a pedal-powered carousel.

John Bourne's daughter, Emily Howland Bourne, donated the **Bourne library's original building** in 1897. The 1897 building, served as the library until 1985 when it was moved to the former Frances Stowell Grammar School. The old building has been repurposed as the Jonathan Bourne Historical Center, housing town archives and the local historic society. It was listed on the National Register of Historic Places in 2013.

The **Bournedale Village School** is a historic school building at 29 Herring Pond Road in Bourne. Built in 1897, it was the last one-room schoolhouse built by the town, and is one of the few surviving 19th-century schoolhouses in all of Barnstable County. It was listed on the National Register of Historic Places in 2013.

The **Cape Cod Canal Railroad Bridge** was built by the Public Works Administration as part of the New Deal and it replaced a bascule (swing) bridge that had been built in 1910.

On the **Sagamore Bridge** there is a six-foot wide sidewalk for pedestrian and bicycle access on the east side of the bridge. The sidewalk is slightly raised, but there is no fence or barrier between it and car traffic, so cyclists are recommended to walk their bicycle. The bridge road is plowed in winter, although the sidewalk is sometimes unplowed and unpassable. The **Sagamore and the Bourne bridges** to the Cape are sometimes closed for safety during high winds.

The **railroad train** that carries waste from Yarmouth to an incinerator in Rochester is called either "energy train" or "trash train" depending on who is describing it. Many of the communities on Cape Cod use this train to dispose of their trash.

Bourne Bridge replaces an earlier 1911 drawbridge, and the original drawbridge's approaches are still accessible. The current structure was built to accommodate the widening of the canal and construction was completed in 1935.

Between 1967 and 1977, 36 persons were recorded as having died by suicide from the **Bourne and Sagamore bridges**, and another 24 had attempted but either survived or were apprehended. In 1983, higher fences were installed. In the period after the new fencing was installed (1984-2021), seven persons are known to have died by suicide from the bridges, and between 2013-2021, two attempts were prevented.

Cape Cod Canal has bike and walking paths on both sides of the 7-mile-long canal.

Bourne Scenic Park was founded in 1951 as an area for picnics and camping, with 200 campsites. From its inception, the park has more than doubled in size to its current 439 sites, 408 of which are electric with newly added Cabins & Lodges. It is located beneath the Bourne Bridge along the canal and is a perfect location for those seeking to enjoy the canal and its many activities.

Footprints Cafe is a black-owned, woman-owned bookstore and coffee shop. A warm, cozy inviting space to enjoy while choosing the perfect book, it is a place where inclusion and diversity are honored. A bookstore where the spotlight is on people and authors of color, Footprints Café is where you go "to lose your mind and find your soul."

The **Cape Cod Canal area** covers over 1,655 acres of land on 23 shoreline miles, with 575 water acres. One of the best places to bike, rollerblade, walk, or jog on its immaculate and wide paved pathway.

The Museums at Aptucxet is a 12 acre campus on the banks of the Cape Cod Canal in Bourne, The property also features the 19th-century Gray Gables Railroad Station, which was built to serve **President Grover Cleveland** during his second term and now functions as a mini museum of Cleveland's connection to the area.

With the signing of the first private commercial contract in English-speaking North America, **Aptucxet** became the first private commercial enterprise using a local currency known as **wampum,** a polished fragment of a hard-shell clam usually containing a purple color and shaped in a cylindrical form. The signing also launched what is now the world's leading economic force: the American Free Enterprise System.

Butterflies of Cape Cod is a native butterfly sanctuary in Bourne. They offer a beautiful indoor habitat where butterflies fly free.

Massachusetts National Cemetery is a U.S. National Cemetery in Bourne, adjacent to the Otis Air National Guard Base. As of 2021, over 78,000 have been interred there.

All About Brewster

Brewster /ˈbruːstər/ is a town in Barnstable County, Massachusetts, Barnstable County being coextensive with Cape Cod. The population of Brewster was 10,318 at the 2020 census.

Brewster is "twinned" with the town of Budleigh Salterton in the United Kingdom.

Brewster was first settled in 1656 as a northeastern parish of the town of Harwich. The town separated from Harwich as the northern, more wealthy parish in 1693, and was officially incorporated as its own town in 1803 when the less wealthy citizens of Harwich were upset that the town's institutions were all on Brewster's main street (now Route 6A), including the town hall and churches. Brewster was named in honor of Elder William Brewster, the first religious leader of the Pilgrims at Plymouth Colony. The town's history grew around Stony Brook, where the first water-powered grist and woolen mill in the country was founded in the late 17th century. There were many rich sea captains in the town, who built many of the mansions and stately homes which now constitute the town's inns and bed-and-breakfasts. Most notable of these are the Brewster Historical Society Capt. Elijah Cobb House on Lower Road, Crosby Mansion on Crosby Lane by Crosby Beach, and the Captain Freeman Inn on Breakwater Road.

The Brewster Store came into being in 1866. Originally a church with a steeple, the church building, and the property were purchased for "one dollar" by William W. Knowles, who ran the Crocker and Kimball Store down the road. Knowles removed the church steeple and extended the front porch, adding wide store front windows. In addition, the ceiling of the first floor was raised to right below the three large church windows on both the east and west walls, thereby creating a more spacious first floor. When Knowles opened his new general store in 1866, it was one of six in Brewster. He reserved the large second floor for plays, dances, and social events, and during his tenure it was known as "THE HALL."

People of Significance – Brewster

Brewster was named in honor of **Elder William Brewster**, the first religious leader of the Pilgrims at Plymouth Colony. William Brewster (1566/67 - April 10, 1644) was an English official and Mayflower passenger in 1620. In Plymouth Colony, by virtue of his education and existing stature with those immigrating from the Netherlands, Brewster, a Brownist (or Puritan Separatist), became senior elder and the leader of the community.

Elijah Cobb was born in Brewster July 4, 1768. He first commanded the ship Jane; later commands included the Monsoon, Paragon, and Ten Brothers. He is arguable Brewster's most famous sea captain; traveling around the world and landing in France in time to run afoul of its Revolution. His ship's cargo of rice and flour was confiscated to feed the starving populace; he engineered a private meeting with Robespierre, and later witnessed his beheading. He went on to run rum off the coast of Ireland and engage in the gold and ivory trade in Africa. During the War of 1812 his ship was captured and he became a prisoner of war, a prisoner exchange finally allowing his return to Brewster.

In the late 1700s Captain Cobb wrote home from sea: "My pertner [sic] in life's voyage has run me in debt for a Cape Cod farm." He bought the farm from Thankful Freeman, widow of David Freeman, and built his home in 1799, moving in on New Year's Day 1800. The property then stretched all the way to Cape Cod Bay.

Captain Cobb retired from the sea to his farm in 1820, serving in many civic posts in town until his death, leaving behind not only the lovely home on Lower Road but a rare record of a sea captain's life in a diary published by the Yale University Press. (For sale in the Museum Gift Shop)

Captain Cobb died in 1848 and is buried in the Brewster Cemetery on Lower Road. Today the National Register of Historic

Places lists Captain Cobb as the first person of historical interest in the Old King's Highway District.

The Captain Elijah Cobb House at 739 Lower Road is one of Brewster's most historically significant buildings.

Captain William Freeman located his home convenient to the packet landing. Capt. Freeman commanded the famed clipper ships Kingfisher, the Maine, the Undaunted, the Monsoon, the Mogul, the Ocean King, and Jabez Howes. Unlike most of his other Brewster compatriots, he also captained three steamers: Zenobia, Palmyra, and Edward Everett.

Old Higgins Farm Windmill is a historic Smock windmill off Old King's Highway at Drummer Boy Park in Brewster. The windmill, built in 1795, last ground grain around 1900 and was added to the National Historic Register of Historic Places in 1975.

Do You Know – Brewster?

The Brewster Book Store is a full-service independent book store filled to the brim with books, toys, games, greeting cards, stationery, unique gifts, and so much more. The store is proud of its collection of Cape Cod books, its extensive children's section, and its wide selection of hardcover and paperback books for readers of all tastes and ages. Check its website for always interesting events.

The Brewster Flats measure approximately 12,000 acres at low tide and are the largest flats in North America. This unique area extends over nine miles along the coastline from Brewster to North Eastham. When the tide goes out this natural phenomenon creates a spectacular, naturally reoccurring recreational area. If you hike out to the middle of the Bay, you can see where the original wooden packet landing was built to allow packet ships to come into Breakwater landing where they ferried cargo and travelers to and from Boston.

Brewster is best known for its **flats fishing** for striped bass. In this section of Cape Cod Bay sand flats extend for miles during low tide. It is highly recommended that you watch the weather and tide, so you do not get stuck on a sand bar, or in a fog bank with the tide coming in.

The Grist Mill is the only remaining structure from Brewster's Factory Village, a bustling 19th Century industrial area. The restored mill is open every Saturday in the summer. Visitors can see the water wheel in motion and purchase fresh ground corn meal. The Grist Mill is the only remaining structure from Brewster's Factory Village, a bustling 19th Century industrial area.

The upstairs **Grist Mill Museum** features artifacts of 19th Century Cape Cod life, weaving demonstrations and more. Visitors strolling the footpaths might happen upon basking turtles, spot a heron flying overhead, see dragonflies hovering over the mill pond, or see a variety of fish in the brook. Brewster Grist Mill & Museum is also a herring run; a very popular destination in late March and early April.

Many people wonder why, in these gender-neutral days, the **"Brewster Ladies' Library"** is still used. In the 1970s an objection was raised to the name because of the possibility of misinterpretation – that men were not allowed. However, in an overwhelming vote at the annual library meeting, the decision was made to go with history and keep the name. In 1999, "Your Community Library" was added to the name to avoid confusion.

The present **Mansion at Ocean Edge** used to be called the Fieldstone Hall and was built in 1890 by Samuel Mayo Nickerson for his son Roland and his wife Addie. Nickerson was a native of the area and a Chicago liquor distiller who made a fortune as one of the founding officers of the First National Bank of Chicago. The building was destroyed in a great fire in 1906 and the existing Victorian-style mansion, a major feature of the Ocean Edge Resort, was rebuilt in 1912 and is listed on the National Register of Historic Places. Legend has it that Addie's ghost still wanders the hallways, eternally heartbroken over the loss of her husband and desperately clinging to her mansion. The land composing the **Nickerson State Park** was once part of this estate.

In 1656, **Brewster** was settled as a parish town of Harwich. Brewster separated from Harwich in 1693 due to tensions with the less wealthy part of Harwich in the south.

The **Crosby mansion** is a three story, thirty-five room monument to romance. It is the legacy of a man, Albert Crosby, who went west to Chicago to make his fortune selling untaxed medicinal alcohol to the Union Army and returned to Brewster with a bride 20 years his junior, for whom he built the mansion called Tawasentha.

The **Brewster Store's** history began in 1852 when it was originally constructed as a church. In the 1860s, the church was purchased for just one dollar by William K. Knowles. He transformed the building into a general store by removing the church steeple and adding bright, storefront windows. The second floor was dubbed "The Hall" and held local plays, dances, and social events.

By 1809, sixty thousand feet of **salt works** lined Brewster's shore. The saltworks industry reached its peak in the 1830s. The salts works provided such a huge value in the early 1800s that during the war of 1812 a British naval commander threatened to blow up the salt works unless the town paid a $4,000 bribe; it was paid.

Some of Brewster's rich history can be found in the circa 1770 First Parish Brewster Universalist Unitarian Church whose pews are marked with the names of ninety-nine famous **Brewster sea-captains**.

In 1850 there were **fifty clipper ship captains** living in Brewster. Many started their career by shipping out as a young boy on the clipper ships. The ships left Brewster Landing to go to Boston to pick up their cargo and from there they travelled the world.

Use of clipper ships ended in 1860 when the Railroad came to Cape Cod and the Suez Canal opened.

Drummer Boy Park is a hidden little park by the ocean that features a picturesque windmill, plenty of grass and fresh sea breezes. The windmill was built in 1795 and moved to the park. There is a playground at the park, and events, such as arts and crafts fairs and outdoor concerts, are frequently held here in the warmer months.

The **John Wing Trail** is a beautiful seaside loop trail in Brewster that will take you through a salt marsh. It is 2.2 miles long and starts behind the Cape Cod Natural History Museum. A solar calendar on Wing's Island along the trail is interesting to check out.

The Cape Cod Natural History Museum owns four hundred acres of land in Stony Brook Valley and Brewster conservation land adjacent to the museum, including Wing's Island, the salt marsh, and the beach along Cape Cod Bay between Quivett and Paine's Creeks.

Hall of Famer **Tony Gwynn and his son Tony Gwynn, Jr.**, both played for the Brewster Whitecaps of the Cape Cod Baseball league.

The Brewster Flats, are created by the ebb and flow of the daily tides when the waters recede out of Cape Cod Bay over one mile to reveal sandbars, clam beds and tidal pools teeming with sea life.

In the early 1800s the land-based production of salt grew quite large, with over 60 **salt works** scattered throughout the town.

All About Chatham

Chatham (IPA: ˈ[tʃætəm]) is a town in Barnstable County. Chatham is located at the southeast tip of Cape Cod and has historically been a fishing community. First settled by the English in 1664, the township was originally called Monomoit based on the indigenous population's term for the region.

Native American tribes who lived in the area before European colonization included the Nauset, specifically the Manomoy or Monomoy people. The expansive lands over which they roamed were known to them as Manamoyik or Monomoit.

Explorer Samuel de Champlain landed here in October 1606 at a place he christened "Port Fortuné," where he contacted (and skirmished with) the Nauset. Twelve years later another group of Europeans gave it the name "Sutcliffe's Inlets."

The arrival of English colonists began about 1656 when William Nickerson, an English emigrant working as a land surveyor and weaver in Yarmouth on Cape Cod made the first land purchase from Sachem Mitoguazone of the Monomoyicks. Nickerson failed to get permission for the purchase (a requirement at that time) from the Plymouth General Court. As a result, the Court confiscated his land except for a 100-acre Homestead. But, after 10 to 12 years of litigation, he regained ownership. With additional purchases, he ultimately owned all of what is now Chatham with the exception of some land east of Old Harbor Road which had been reserved for the Monomoyicks. In 1664 Nickerson settled his family on the west side of Ryder's Cove.

By the 1690s, 17 families lived in Chatham, and that number slowly grew to 50 families in the early 1700s while the native population dwindled to 50-70.

The town was incorporated on June 11, 1712, at which point it was renamed after Chatham, Kent, England. Its territory expanded with the annexation of Strong Island and its vicinity on February 7, 1797.

It wasn't until after the Revolutionary War that Chatham stabilized and grew. Industries such as fish export, shipbuilding, and salt production brought life to the economy. Agriculture, fishing, whaling, and maritime enterprises flourished. In 1830, during the height of salt works production, the population was 2,130.

Located at the "elbow" of Cape Cod, the community became a shipping, fishing, and whaling center. Chatham's early prosperity would leave it with a considerable number of 18th century buildings, whose charm helped it develop into a popular summer resort.

The population was 6,594 at the 2020 census and can swell to 25,000 during the summer months. There are four villages that comprise the town, those being Chatham (CDC), South Chatham, North Chatham, and West Chatham.

Chatham is home to the Chatham Lighthouse, which was established by President Thomas Jefferson in 1808 to protect the ships circling the Cape. The 1808 towers were replaced in 1841 by twin brick towers that were eventually lost to erosion. The pair were rebuilt in 1877 out of cast iron across the street from its original location, where the light is today. The northern of the two was moved to Eastham to become the Nauset Light in 1923, when the northern tower was declared surplus. Today, the keeper's house is home to a Coast Guard station which patrols the waters of the Atlantic and Nantucket Sound from Wellfleet to West Yarmouth.

Secrets of the history of Chatham Borough and the Township have recently been revealed along the banks of the Passaic River. Young archaeologists from Drew University have collected fascinating artifacts from the site where George Shepard Page built the Stanley Felt Mill, housing for immigrant workers, and a store stocked with creature comforts from their homelands.

> "I was a writer on Cape Cod."
>
> Author: Kurt Vonnegut Jr.

People of Significance – Chatham

Samuel de Champlain (Frenc: [samɥɛl də ʃɑ̃plɛ̃]; c. 13 August 1567– 25 December 1635) was a French colonist, navigator, cartographer, draftsman, soldier, explorer, geographer, ethnologist, diplomat, and chronicler. He made between 21 and 29 trips across the Atlantic Ocean, and founded Quebec, and New France, on 3 July 1608. An important figure in Canadian history, Champlain created the first accurate coastal map during his explorations, and founded various colonial settlements. He was the first European to step foot in Chatham.

Born into a family of sailors, Champlain began exploring North America in 1603, under the guidance of his uncle, François Gravé Du Pont. After 1603, Champlain's life and career consolidated into the path he would follow for the rest of his life.

From 1604 to 1607, he participated in the exploration and creation of the first permanent European settlement north of Florida, Port Royal, Acadia (1605).

In 1608, he established the French settlement that is now Quebec City.

In 1605 and 1606, Champlain explored the North American coast as far south as Cape Cod, searching for sites for a permanent settlement. Minor skirmishes with the resident Nausets dissuaded him from the idea of establishing one near present-day Chatham. He named the area Mallebar ("bad bar").

Tisquantum (/tɪsˈkwɒntəm/; c. 1585 – late November 1622), more commonly known as Squanto (/ˈskwɒntoʊ/), was a member of the Patuxet tribe best known for being an early liaison between the Native American population in Southern New England and the Mayflower Pilgrims who made their settlement at the site of Tisquantum's former summer village. The Patuxet tribe had lived on the western coast of Cape Cod Bay, but they were wiped out by an epidemic infection, likely brought by previous European explorers.

Tisquantum was kidnapped by English explorer Thomas Hunt who carried him to Spain, where he sold him in the city of Málaga. He was among a number of captives bought by local monks who focused on their education and evangelization. Tisquantum eventually traveled to England, where he may have met Pocahontas, a Native American from Virginia, in 1616–1617. He then returned to America in 1619 to his native village, only to find that his tribe had been wiped out by an epidemic infection; Tisquantum was the last of the Patuxets, and went to live with the Wampanoags.

The Mayflower landed in Cape Cod Bay in 1620, and Tisquantum worked to broker peaceable relations between the Pilgrims and the local Pokanokets. He played a key role in the early meetings in March 1621, partly because he spoke English. He then lived with the Pilgrims for 20 months, acting as an interpreter, guide, and advisor. He introduced the settlers to the fur trade and taught them how to sow and fertilize native crops; this proved vital, because the seeds which the Pilgrims had brought from England mostly failed. As food shortages worsened, Plymouth Colony Governor William Bradford relied on Tisquantum to pilot a ship of settlers on a trading expedition around Cape Cod and through dangerous shoals. During that voyage, Tisquantum contracted what Bradford called an "Indian fever." Bradford stayed with him for several days until he died, which Bradford described as a "great loss."

He died in Monomoit, now Chatham.

William Nickerson, founder of Chatham, arrived in Salem in 1637 aboard the ship, John and Dorothy, with four children, his wife, Anne Busby, and her parents. A weaver by trade, he left Norwich, England, to escape the persecution of Bishop Wren of the Church of England against nonconformists. After first settling near Little Bass Pond in Yarmouth, he bargained with Monomoyick tribal sachem, Mattaquason, for a parcel of land at Monomoit (now Chatham) in 1656. A shallop, cloth, several kettles, axes, knives and wampum served as payment. By 1664 William, Anne and eight of their nine children and their families were living in various parts of the 4,000 acres of Monomoit. However, because it was illegal to purchase tribal lands directly, it wasn't until 1682 with a payment of ninety pounds and a Plymouth Colony Court settlement that the purchase was made legal. William was active in both civil and religious affairs. He called his family together on the Sabbath to read and explain the scriptures and later became a lay leader and founder of the village church.

Eighth generation descendant, **William Emery Nickerson**, inventor of the Gillette safety razor, gathered 300 Nickersons together in Chatham in 1897 to form a family genealogical society. For the next 30 years, correspondence was collected from scattered Nickerson descendants all around the United States and Canada. Today the Nickerson Family Association continues to update and add to genealogy records. Award winning volumes have been published reflecting years of research which have been devoted to Nickerson genealogy.

The Nickerson House serves as a genealogical research center and headquarters of the Nickerson Family Association. The relocated early 19th century Caleb Nickerson House operates as a period restoration and living history teaching museum.

Joseph Crosby Lincoln (February 13, 1870 – March 10, 1944) was an American author of novels, poems, and short stories, many set in a fictionalized Cape Cod.

Lincoln was born in 1870 in Brewster, and his mother moved the family to Chelsea, Massachusetts, a manufacturing city outside Boston, after the death of his father. Lincoln's literary career celebrating "old Cape Cod" can partly be seen as an attempt to return to an Eden from which he had been driven by family tragedy. His literary portrayal of Cape Cod can also be understood as a pre-modern haven occupied by individuals of old Yankee stock which was offered to readers as an antidote to an America that was undergoing rapid modernization, urbanization, immigration, and industrialization. Lincoln was a Republican and a Universalist.

Lincoln's work frequently appeared in popular magazines such as the Saturday Evening Post and The Delineator. Lincoln was aware of contemporary naturalist writers, such as Frank Norris and Theodore Dreiser, who used American literature to plumb the depths of human nature, but he rejected this literary exercise. Lincoln claimed that he was satisfied "spinning yarns" that made readers feel good about themselves and their neighbors. Six films and a short were based on his work.

Upon becoming successful, Lincoln summered in Chatham. In Chatham, he lived in a shingle-style house named "Crosstrees" that was located on a bluff overlooking the Atlantic Ocean.

Ocean view from the front steps of Chatham Bars Inn

"On Cape Cod, great white shark stocks have been growing, or at least becoming more concentrated, because of the multiplying numbers of seals around Monomoy Island. We are fortunate to have such abundance of these sharks in our own waters. Around the globe, we are killing in excess of 100 million sharks each year."

Author: Brian Skerry

Do You Know – Chatham?

During Chatham's early history, an eight-mile sandbar that runs through Chatham Harbor destroyed so many ships that sailors began to say it was haunted by the stallion of a drowned mooncusser who lured sailors to their demise. To keep ships off these dangerous shoals, the town of Chatham erected a small lighthouse on a crumbling bluff overlooking the harbor inlet. **Chatham Light**, completed in 1808, was just the second lighthouse on the Cape.

The first **reforesting project** in America took place on Great Hill in 1821 when Selectmen had pine trees and beach grass planted to prevent erosion and to keep sand from blowing over the village.

The town includes two narrow strips of land which serve as a barrier between the Atlantic and the mainland; the northern of these is the southern part of the **Cape Cod National Seashore**.

There are **several islands**, including Strong Island, Tern Island (which is a sanctuary), Morris Island, Stage Island, and Monomoy Island, a 7.25-mile-long (11.67 km) island south of the corner of the town which is home to the Monomoy National Wildlife Refuge. Monomoy Island is technically two islands South Monomoy Island and North Monomoy Island.

Erosion has changed the region over the years—for example, an island named Slut's Bush once existed until it vanished under water by the mid-19th century.

In December 2021, the **median listing home price** in Chatham, MA was $1.5M, trending up 19.6% year-over-year. The median listing home price per square foot was $644. The median home sold price was $1.1M.

Chatham, was home to the largest ship-to-shore radiotelegraph station in the United States, established in 1921 by the Radio Corporation of America. For most of the 20th century, the station was known to mariners worldwide as Chatham Radio, with call letters WCC. The history of the **Chatham Radio** site began prior to World War I with the work of radio pioneer Guglielmo Marconi and the Marconi Wireless Telegraph Company of America. In 1912, American Marconi continued to pursue the promise of intercontinental wireless with construction of five great high-power stations on the east and west coasts. Construction of the Massachusetts station, with transmitting facilities in Marion and receiving facilities in Chatham, began in the spring of 1914.

Windmills were once an integral part of life in Chatham. There were about eleven wind-powered grist mills located in the town from the early 1700s through the 1800s, with six to nine in operation during any one time. (There were also dozens of smaller windmills that pumped sea water to the saltworks located along the town's shores.) The **Chatham Windmill**, also known as the Col. Benjamin Godfrey Mill, was one of the last of the town's grist mills to be built. Today only two of these historic mills exist in Chatham and only the Godfrey Mill is open to the public.

The **Atwood Museum,** in Chatham, is a property of the Chatham Historical Society which, in 1926, purchased the property of Captain Joseph Atwood (1720–1794) to protect the property and to display and preserve articles and documents related to Chatham's history.

The **lighthouse turret** from Chatham's famous Twin Light which guided shipping from 1808 to 1923 can be seen at the Atwood Museum.

The **Caleb Nickerson House Museum** is a "working" museum of life on Cape Cod in the early 19th century. It features a beehive oven, period woodwork and a Colonial kitchen vegetable and herb garden.

The Chatham Railroad Museum was the former depot which was the stepping off – and on – point for riders of the old Chatham Railroad, which served the town with a seven-mile strip of railway for about fifty years from 1887 to 1937. The Chatham Railroad Museum exhibits model trains and train artifacts in a former depot dating from 1887.

By 1925 there were more than 8 hotels in town, and of the approximately 900 dwellings almost half were seasonal residences, a ratio that continues today. The development of Chatham as a **summer resort** brought with it the establishment of golf clubs, a beach club, and yacht clubs.

The Navy built an **Air Station** on 36 acres at the eastern end of Eastward Point, which operated until 1923. It was there that the "NC-4 flying boat" stopped for repairs before making the first trans-Atlantic flight.

The Chatham Bars Inn was originally built as a hunting lodge by Charles Hardy of Boston. He specifically designed the structure in the popular style of New England "Shingle" architecture, which gave the location its iconic eloquence and grandeur. Taking several months to complete, the "Chatham Bars Inn" debuted for the first time in 1914. Guests marveled at the soundproofed guestroom, as well as private bathrooms equipped with both fresh and saltwater tubs. Since its opening, it has expanded its number of rooms and suites and guest amenities that take full advantage of its ocean views and continues to rank as the premier inn on Cape Cod.

The Chatham Fish Pier deck is viewable via Chatham webcam. The deck hosts 3,000 people a day in the summer who wait to watch the fishing boats unload their catch.

Yellow Umbrella Books offers new and gently used books. It offers a full range of books from the most popular to esoteric titles that interest a few. You will find a good selection of children's books and books about Cape Cod, and a staff that is knowledgeable and courteous.

The **Atlantic White Shark Conservancy** offers an in-depth look at one of the ocean's most magnificent and misunderstood species: the Great White Shark! Through interactive exhibits, videos, and displays, the center offers many ways to learn about groundbreaking research and one of Cape Cod's most captivating summer residents.

The Atwood Museum offers a variety of methods to research your family's history; assistance to create an oral history and scan and digitize your family photos.

Where the Sidewalk Ends Bookstore is a mother-daughter-owned bookstore in a welcoming, two-story "antique" barn with an attached Children's Annex full of educational books and imagination-enriching toys. A comfortable fireside and outdoor seating provide relaxing places for browsing, sipping coffee, and enjoying a friendly ambiance. A courteous and knowledgeable staff provide excellent service.

> "On the wall hung a picture of an ugly old Cape Cod house. His friends said, 'Why do you have that ugly thing hanging there?' and Bull said, 'I like it because it's ugly.'"
>
> Author: Jack Kerouac

All About Dennis

Dennis is a town in Barnstable County, located near the center of Cape Cod. The population was 14,674 at the 2020 census.

The town encompasses five distinct villages, each of which has its own post office. These constituent villages are Dennis (including North Dennis), Dennis Port, East Dennis, South Dennis, and West Dennis.

Dennis was first settled by Europeans in 1639, by John Crowe (later Crowell), Antony Thacher, and Thomas Howes, as part of the town of Yarmouth. It was known then as the East Precinct. The original inhabitants who preceded English settlers called the northern sections of town Nobscuesset, Sesuit, and Quivet.

The town officially separated and incorporated in 1793. It was named after resident minister, Rev. Josiah Dennis. There was not enough land for farming, so seafaring became the town's major industry in its early history, centered around the Shiverick Shipyard.

Fishing continued to be the principal industry of the town for three quarters of a century. In 1889 the fishing and coasting vessels registered from Dennis had a total tonnage of 6,955. The fertile Atlantic and other waters have furnished broad maritime fields of labor in which Dennis has increased its wealth and importance more than in agriculture, but during the past twenty years the bogs of the town have been redeemed for the cultivation of cranberries, and the town now has a high position in this branch of industry. The town still had in 1889 over sixty vessels of various tonnage, including nine three-masters, engaged in the coast and fishing trade

Currently, Dennis is a popular seaside resort town, notable for its stately colonial mansions along the northern Cape Cod Bay coastline, and its picturesque, warm-water beaches along the southern Nantucket Sound.

People of Significance – Dennis

Josiah Dennis, born in 1694 in Wenham and Harvard graduate, was ordained as the first minister of the Second Parish of Yarmouth on June 22, 1727. His home was a c.1693 house refurbished by his parish, now known as the 1736 Josiah Dennis Manse Museum because of a later addition.

Josiah married twice, burying his first wife, Bathsheba, in 1745. He married Phebe, who outlived him by 10 years. He had nine children, two sons and five daughters. Six children died before Josiah, leaving three daughters, one of whom would marry.

He left a hand written will and a household inventory. In Yarmouth church records, there is an acceptance to preach letter, a record of his being received by the church and bits of sermons. There are no sketches or paintings or descriptions of his likeness. At the Manse there is a desk he may have made as he was an apprenticed carpenter. At his death his will notes the value of his books at 30 pounds and the value of his wearing apparel at 16.94 pounds.

It seems Reverend Josiah Dennis was kind, caring, dedicated to his parish and able to offer his parishioners a wry sense of humor. He considered himself a "friend and servant." Reverend Dennis is buried in Dennis Village Cemetery and the town is fortunate to have been named in his honor.

His church was a small wooden meeting house on the edge of what would eventually become Dennis Village Cemetery.

John Sears (1744-1817) (colloquially known as Sleepy John Sears) was a salt producer in Massachusetts Bay Colony.

He was born in Yarmouth on the neck of Cape Cod and spent most of his life as a sea captain. He was known as Sleepy John because of his habit of falling asleep during the day.

In the years leading up to the Revolutionary War the colonists were concerned about the loss of salt imports from overseas which were vital for the preservation of meat and fish.

To solve the problem John Sears adopted a solution based on the evaporation of seawater in large wooden vats, which he constructed near his Cape Cod home in Dennis. The process was inefficient and unrewarding at first, but he improved it by making the vats leakproof, providing moveable covers to keep out the rain and installing a salvaged bilge pump to draw water directly from the sea via lead lined wooden pipes. He profited considerably both from his production improvements and from the increase in the price of salt from fifty cents a bushel to $8 by the time the war finished in 1783. In 1785 he built a windmill to pump the water automatically from the sea.

He died in 1817 a relatively rich man and was buried in nearby West Brewster. His epitaph is inscribed "John Sears, Inventor of the Salt Works, Aged 72 yrs." He had married his wife Phebe Sears on December 26, 1771, in Yarmouth and had nine children.

By the time of his death many other local people had followed him into vat-based salt production and by 1837 there were in excess of 650 saltworks on Cape Cod alone, an industry that prospered until cheaper alternative sources became available in the 1800s. He is nowadays jointly commemorated, together with John Winthrop, Jr., by the annual award from the Chemists' Club and Chemical Heritage Foundation of the Winthrop-Sears Medal, which recognizes entrepreneurial achievement in the chemical field.

Edward Gelsthorpe (June 14, 1921 – September 12, 2009) was an American marketing executive and a resident of East Dennis. He used his creative skills to build markets for new products such as Ban roll-on deodorant at Bristol-Myers, Cranapple juice for the Ocean Spray cooperative, and Manwich canned sloppy joe sauce for Hunt-Wesson. While CEO of Ocean Spray he was able to oversee the development of several brand extensions, including its blockbuster Cranapple and other fresh and frozen fruit juice mixes, as well as a cranberry-orange relish. Sales doubled with these new products as well as efforts to promote the use of cranberry juice in mixed drinks, all leading to his nickname of "Cranapple Ed."

Do You Know – Dennis?

The Cape Playhouse, in northern Dennis, is one of the oldest summer theatres in the United States (it is not clear which theatre is the oldest, as many make this claim), and among the best known.

The actress **Bette Davis** was "discovered" while working at The Cape Playhouse as an usher.

The **Cape Cinema** was founded in 1930 by Edna B. Tweedy and Raymond Moore, three years after Moore founded the Cape Playhouse. The building's exterior was designed by Alfred Easton Poor and modeled after the South Congregational Church in Centerville.

Johnny Kelley Recreation area in South Dennis is a 25-acre park with multiple recreational facilities, named in honor of world-renowned marathon runner and local resident, Johnny Kelley. He was a member of the 1936 and 1948 Olympic teams and ran the Boston Marathon more than 50 times, winning in 1935 and 1945.

Local legend tells us that in the 19th century, an aged Nobscusset Indian lived in a cave beneath a tremendous pile of granite, aka **Hokum Rock**, left by retreating glaciers in what is now Dennis village. Whenever someone approached the rock, the Indian would shout, "Who come?" providing the rock and the road the name Hokum.

The **Nobscussett Conservation Area** (usually called "Indian Lands") provides easy hiking trails and views along the protected shores of Bass River, where the Nobscussetts had spent their winters. The reasons the Indigenous people spent their winters there were the area offered shelter from the north winds, good water from springs, and plentiful fish and shellfish. They continued to reside here as late as 1778.

The **Bass River** on Cape Cod forms a border between the towns of Yarmouth and Dennis and was once considered as the site of a canal that would have bisected the Cape.

Scargo Tower began as a tourist observatory in 1874. Made of wood, it was destroyed in a gale two years later. Rebuilt again of wood, it burned in 1900; the present cobblestone tower opened in 1901. The 30-foot-high tower is located atop the highest hill in the mid-Cape. Indian legends tell of the making of both Scargo Hill and Scargo Lake. Views may be seen of the entire lower cape to Provincetown, and as far west as Plymouth. The Tower is owned and operated by the Town of Dennis.

There is a plaque placed on a stone on a rise next to the Town parking lot on Shiverick Rd. in South Dennis that commemorates the **Shiverick Ship Yard** which launched its first schooner in 1815. Subsequently more schooners and eight clipper ships were built. The clipper ships traveled the world.

In 1920 the **bogs** of the town were rehabilitated for the cultivation of cranberries, and the town prospered in this branch of industry. The town still had over sixty vessels of various tonnage, including nine three-masters, engaged in the coast and fishing trade.

Chapin Memorial Beach, which was previously known as Black Flats for its black sands and extensive tidal flats, was named in honor of George H. Chapin, a real estate developer who donated the land to the Town after World War II. The area leading to Chapin Beach has alternatively been known as Little Italy and Little Taunton for the Italian immigrants who came by way of Taunton, Massachusetts, in the late 1800s to build the railroad on Cape Cod. Many streets in the area, such as Squadrilli Way, Dr. Boterro Road, Spadoni Road, and Angelo Road, as well as Lombardi Heights, were named for Italians.

Dennis Port was named by Thomas Howes, the village's first postmaster, in 1850. Previously it had been known as Crooks Neck, after Samuel Crook, a Native American who sold the land to English settlers in the 17th century. The name changed to Crookers Neck before becoming Dennis Port.

On the Harwich line is **White Pond**, so named because of the way the light hits the water. It was formerly known as Aunt Lizzie Robbins Pond, named for a member of the Robbins family of Harwich, who arrived on the Cape in the early 1700s.

Swan Pond took its name from the Algonquin word sowan, meaning south. It is also known as Jamies Pond, after James Chase.

In **South Dennis** the area of Scargo Lake and Scargo Hill in Dennis are associated with ancient Native American folklore. When viewed from Scargo Tower atop the hill, Scargo Lake appears to be in the shape of a fish. The lake is a glacial kettle pond and the hills on the northern side of the town are moraines, formed from gravel and debris left by the glacier, much like a conveyor belt.

The **Indian Burial Ground** is located above the shores of Scargo Lake. In 1829 it was enclosed with a stone and iron fence for $160 and yet there are no headstones to define burials, which is in keeping with early Native American tradition.

West Dennis Beach was once known as Davis Beach, and the road that runs along the length of the beach is Davis Beach Road. Charles Henry Davis sold the beach to the Town in the early 1900s. Davis once transported and combined seven houses into a single mansion on the other side of the Bass River in South Yarmouth, giving it the name The House of Seven Chimneys.

At the east end of the beach is the Lighthouse Inn on Lighthouse Road, where a lighthouse was built in 1855 and was in service until 1914. Recently, the **West Dennis Light** has been restored as a private aid to navigation and operates during the summer months.

West Dennis is indeed west of Dennisport and south of South Dennis. East Dennis is north of South Dennis, and Dennis is on the western shore, to the west of East Dennis. **Got it?**

Chapin Memorial Beach, which was previously known as Black Flats for its black sands and extensive tidal flats, was named in honor of George H. Chapin, a real estate developer who donated the land to the Town after World War II. Chase Garden Creek empties into Cape Cod Bay at Chapin Beach, and serves as a boundary between Dennis and Yarmouth. It was named for the Chase family, settlers who were on the Cape by 1638.

Glendon Road, and the beach named for the street, took their name from Hubert Glendon, a Marine officer who served as the Columbia University rowing coach after World War II, and who donated the beach to the village. To the west is Peter Hagis Beach, which is located on land donated by his widow.

All About Eastham

Eastham (/ˈiːsthæm/) is a town in Barnstable County, Massachusetts, Barnstable County being coextensive with Cape Cod. The population was 5,752 at the 2020 census.

Originally inhabited by the Nauset tribe, Eastham was the site where in 1620 a hunting expedition landed, comprised from the crew of the sailing vessel Mayflower, which had stopped in Provincetown harbor on Cape Cod Bay after a rough crossing of the Atlantic Ocean, which led to the first encounter of the Pilgrims and the local Nauset people at First Encounter Beach.

Europeans would not settle the area, however, until 1644. The original lands included what are now the towns of Truro, Wellfleet, Eastham, Orleans and a small portion of Chatham. Eastham town was officially incorporated in 1651.

Today, Eastham is known as the "Gateway" to the Cape Cod National Seashore, which was founded in 1961 by President John F. Kennedy to protect Cape Cod's coast from erosion and overpopulation. The town is the site of many beaches, both on the Atlantic and on Cape Cod Bay, as well as the Nauset Light, which was moved to the town in 1923 from its old location in Chatham, and the Three Sisters Lighthouses, which have since been moved away from their now-eroded perches on the coast to a field just west of Nauset Light.

People of Significance – Eastham

In 1644 Thomas Prence, **Nicholas Snow**, John Doane, Richard Higgins, Josiah Cooke, Edward Bangs and John Smalley returned to Cape Cod with permission from the Plymouth Colony Court to negotiate with the Nauset tribes and settle on the land. Soon joined by their families, all forty-nine people were the founders of Nauset Plantation. It was the first settlement on Cape Cod to be born exclusively from the original Plymouth Colony. In 1646, the Plymouth Court granted township status to Nauset and, five years later, changed its name to Eastham.

Thomas Prence (c. 1601 – March 29, 1673) was an English born colonist who arrived in the colony of Plymouth in November 1621 on the ship Fortune.

In 1644, the Prence family was one of seven to found a new settlement at Eastham on Cape Cod. The area of the Outer Cape (roughly from Brewster to Provincetown) had been reserved to the Undertakers, and Prence became one of the largest landowners in the area. His holdings included land in what is now Brewster, Harwich, Wellfleet and all of Truro. The land there was fertile, and the town prospered under his guidance. Prence lived there until 1663 when he moved back to Plymouth.

Eastham is the birthplace of **Freeman Hatch**, who in 1853 set the world record for a single-hull wooden sailing vessel from San Francisco around Cape Horn to Boston aboard the clipper ship Northern Light. Fishing and especially farming were early industries in the town, and writers and artists also came to the town.

Gustavus Franklin Swift, born in Sagamore, MA, began his first meatpacking business in Eastham which later moved to Brighton, MA, Albany, NY, and eventually started the meatpacking industry in Chicago.

Do You Know – Eastham?

On November 9, 1620, a ship named the Mayflower, 65 days out from Plymouth, England, made her landfall in the New World at what is now **First Encounter Beach**. Captain Jones, knowing that his Pilgrim passengers were supposed to settle in northern Virginia, headed southeastward. Although he stood well offshore to avoid shoal waters, his ship soon became enmeshed in the worst shoals in the area, Pollock Rip. A miraculous change of wind enabled Jones to sail his ship free of the shoals, and he then turned northward to anchor in Provincetown Harbor, November 11, 1620.

Coast Guard Beach was named the **Great Beach** by Henry David Thoreau.

The **Outer Beach**, or "backside," of Cape Cod has been the notorious graveyard for more than 3,000 ships since the wreck of the Sparrowhawk in 1626. The high cost in lives and property demanded by the sands of Cape Cod, led to the establishment of the **Massachusetts Humane Society** in 1786, the first organization in the nation devoted to the rescue and assistance of shipwrecked mariners. The Humane Society established shelter huts along the coast; later, it built lifeboat stations where surfboats, line-throwing guns, and other lifesaving gear were stored for the use of volunteer crews in times of emergency.

On the outer beach stood the cottage where author **Henry Beston** lived while gathering the material for his book, **The Outermost House**, published in 1928. The book describes life on the outer beach during all four seasons. The house was designed by Henry Beston in 1925. He took meticulous care with every detail because he intended his house to sit on the dune solid as a ship. The sea claimed the house during a storm in 1978.

The original **Three Sisters Lighthouses** were three 15-foot-high masonry towers. The lights soon gained the nickname "The Three Sisters" because from sea they looked like women in white dresses with black hats. Cape Cod shores change quickly. The National Lighthouse Board ordered three new moveable wooden towers to be built thirty feet inland from the original masonry ones. The new towers stood twenty-two feet tall; the lantern housing added an additional seven feet. The old towers were allowed to fall into the Atlantic.

Nauset Light, officially **Nauset Beach Light**, is a restored lighthouse on the Cape Cod National Seashore near Eastham, erected in 1923 using the 1877 tower that was moved here from Chatham. The tower is a cast-iron plate shell lined with brick and stands forty-eight feet (15 m) high. The adjacent oil house (where fuel was stored in the early days) is made of brick and has also been restored. Fully automated, the beacon is a private aid to navigation. The Nauset Light Preservation Society operates, maintains and interprets the site. The tower is located adjacent to Nauset Light Beach.

The **Eastham Windmill**, located in Eastham, is the oldest windmill on Cape Cod. It was constructed by Eastham resident Thomas Paine in Plymouth in 1680. It was first moved to nearby Truro in 1770, then finally to Eastham in 1793. In 1808 the windmill was moved to its present location, near the Eastham Town Hall and the Eastham Public Library.

While repairs are necessary for the Eastham Windmill, over time, a large contribution was made in 1996 by a local Boy Scout whose Eagle Project included both raising the funds and providing the labor to replace several sections of the fencing around this historic landmark. The funding was provided by businesses located within Eastham. The Eastham Windmill has been a long-standing icon to the local **Boy Scouts and Cub Scouts**.

The lighthouse is the **logo** for Cape Cod Potato Chips. It appears on a "Cape Cod & Islands" special license plate which was introduced in 1996 and generates revenue for local counties and development organizations. It was added to the National Register of Historic Places in 1987 as **Nauset Beach Light**.

Eastham is the home to **three museums** maintained by the Eastham Historical Society. The 1869 Schoolhouse Museum is located on Route 6, opposite the National Seashore Center; the 1741 Swift-Daley House, the Antique Tool Museum and the Dill Beach Shack are all on Route 6, adjacent to the Eastham Post Office.

The Town of Eastham manages **seven bay beaches, three fresh water ponds**, Dyer Prince Area and Hemenway Landing.

Doane Rock was left behind by glaciers at the end of the last Ice Age between 12,000 and 18,000 years ago. This giant boulder reaches eighteen feet above the ground and may go as far as twelve feet underground. The total length of the boulder is forty-five feet. The east face of the boulder is well worn by glacial actions as well as countless climbers, and the scramble to the top is both quick and easy.

The seashore's award-winning orientation movie, *Standing Bold*, plays throughout the day at the **Salt Pond Visitor Center**, and other films show on rotation. Films have open captions and assistive listening.

The family-owned and operated **Gift Barn** located on Route 6 has been open since 1976 on the site of what was once a turnip and asparagus farm. With its large souvenir shop, an arcade, miniature golf, and The Red Barn Pizza restaurant just next door, this has been a one-of-a-kind vacation destination for families over the decades. It offers thirty flavors of taffy.

It was in Eastham that **Henry Beston** wrote *The Outermost House.*

The town is discussed at some length in **Henry David Thoreau's** Cape Cod as the somewhat rugged site of one of New England's largest summer "camp-meeting" evangelistic gatherings in the mid-19th century. The gatherings were at times attended by at least "one hundred and fifty ministers, (!) and five thousand hearers" at a site called Millennium Grove, in the northwest part of town. (The area is now a residential neighborhood, the only reminder being Millennium Lane.)

A town employee was dusting off some framed documents in the corner of the archive room at Eastham Historical Society when he found what could be a priceless document. The **piece of paper** was an official **recognition of the appointment of Elijah Knowles** as Justice of the Peace in Barnstable County. Dated June 7, 1785, the document was signed by the Governor of Massachusetts, Samuel Adams.

Nauset Light, the most famous and photographed lighthouse on Cape Cod, is located on the Cape Cod National Seashore. It is an important part of Eastham's cultural and maritime history.

All About Falmouth

Falmouth (/ˈfælməθ/ FAL-məth) is a town in Barnstable County. The population was 32,517 at the 2020 census, making Falmouth the second-largest municipality on Cape Cod after Barnstable. The terminal for the Steamship Authority ferries to Martha's Vineyard is located in the village of Woods Hole in Falmouth. Woods Hole also contains several scientific organizations such as the Woods Hole Oceanographic Institution (WHOI), the Marine Biological Laboratory (MBL), the Woodwell Climate Research Center, NOAA's Woods Hole Science Aquarium, and the scientific institutions' various museums.

There are specific parts of the town of Falmouth, including East Falmouth, Falmouth Village, North Falmouth, Teaticket, West Falmouth, and Woods Hole. Falmouth also encompasses the villages of Hattieville and Waquoit, which are not census-designated places and fall within the village of East Falmouth based on postal service.

Bartholomew Gosnold during an expedition in 1602 landed on what is now Falmouth and named the area for Falmouth, Cornwall, England, his home port.

Falmouth was first settled by English colonists in 1660 and was officially incorporated in 1686. By 1686, there were enough settlers of all types in the area that it was incorporated as the town of Suckanessett. The name is preserved on the town seal.

Early principal activities were farming, salt works, shipping, whaling, and sheep husbandry, which was very popular due to the introduction of Merino sheep and the beginnings of water-powered mills that could process the wool. In 1837, Falmouth averaged about 50 sheep per square mile.

Falmouth saw brief action in the War of 1812, when the area around Falmouth Heights, on its southern coast, was bombarded by several British frigates and ships of the line, and Massachusetts militia hastily entrenched themselves on the beaches to repulse a possible British landing which never came. By 1872, the train had come to Falmouth and Woods Hole, and some of the first summer homes were established. By the late 19th century, cranberries were being cultivated and strawberries were being raised for the Boston market. Large-scale dairying was tried in the early 20th century in interior regions. After the improvement in highways, and thanks in part to the heavy use of neighboring Camp Edwards (now part of Joint Base Cape Cod) during World War II, population growth increased significantly. Large homebuilding booms occurred in the 1970s, followed by others in the 1980s and 1990s.

At the **Museums on the Green** there are:

A 19th century telescope and octant, a model of the Commodore Morris, a whaleship that was built in Woods Hole in 1841, and a cannonball embedded in a tree that we believe the British aboard the HMS Nimrod fired on Falmouth during the War of 1812 tell fascinating stories of the town's past.

A 1928 gavel from the Woman's Christian Temperance Union, a 1939 jukebox which can still play records on occasion, and a lifeboat fixture from the luxury liner Andrea Doria, which sank off Nantucket in 1956, are among the twentieth century artifacts.

A Day in the Life: Falmouth in the Forties. In September 1941, just months before the United States entered World War II, the Falmouth Kiwanis Club made a two-hour video. They chose a variety of locations around town and filmed people doing everyday things. At the time, Falmouth was a small town with a rural feel and a large immigrant population. Nearly 40% of the town was Portuguese, Azorean and/or Cape Verdean. That changed after the war.

Many natural and distinctive features within Falmouth are the result of glaciers. High concentrations of glacial till formed the belt of hills that run along the length of the Cape, known as a moraine

People of Significance – Falmouth

Captain Bartholomew Gosnold obtained backing to attempt to found an English colony in the New World and in 1602 he sailed from Falmouth, Cornwall, in a small Dartmouth bark, the Concord, with thirty-two on board. They intended to establish a colony in New England. Gosnold pioneered a direct sailing route due west from the Azores to what later became New England, arriving in May 1602 at Cape Elizabeth in Maine (Lat. 43 degrees).

On May 14, 1602, Gosnold made landfall off the southern coast of Maine with the purpose of setting up a small fishing outpost of 20 of the crew who would stay the winter. They were there hailed by a "Biscay shallop" containing eight men, who the English discovered were not "Christians" as they had supposed but "savages" of "swart" color who had many European accoutrements and acted boldly among the English.

The next day, on May 15, 1602, he sailed into Provincetown Harbor, where he is credited with naming Cape Cod, for the abundant fish. The captain explored the land and found a young Native boy, wearing copper ear decorations and an apparent willingness to help the Englishman. Continuing down the Atlantic coast of Cape Cod, pivoting on Gilbert's Point, they coasted westward observing numerous Natives on shore, many running after them to gaze.

Gosnold landed on what is now Falmouth and named the area for Falmouth, Cornwall, England, his home port.

He also discovered Martha's Vineyard, which they explored but found seemingly uninhabited. Gosnold named it after his deceased daughter, Martha, and the wild grapes that covered much of the land.

In 1660, fourteen families came by boat from Barnstable to Suckanesset and built their homes on a strip of land between what is now Siders Pond and Salt Pond. They were led by **Isaac Robinson**, who had incurred the wrath of the Barnstable elders by protesting harassment and persecution of Quakers. Settled by families with principles of religious toleration, Falmouth remained tolerant. There is no record of Quaker persecution here, and the Native Americans also were generally treated fairly. Isaac Robinson and his companions built a permanent community; many of their descendants are still living in Falmouth and their memory is perpetuated in many of the street names of the modern town.

Jonathan Hatch, one of the original proprietors, developed strong ties of mutual friendship and respect with the local Wampanoag tribe. It was a point of pride with the settlers that all land for settlement was bought rather than taken from the Indians, and that Cape Cod Indians did not join other New England tribes in the bloody uprising of 1675 known as King Phillip's War.

John Weeks established a farm in Falmouth in 1679 that was operated by his descendants for nearly three centuries and was known as Peterson Farm. They raised cattle and sheep and planted orchards and a variety of crops. After the farm was abandoned, it was purchased by John Pederson, a local businessman. In 1998 the Town bought the property.

Charles Bennett Ray (December 25, 1807 – August 15, 1886) was a prominent African-American abolitionist, minister, owner and editor of the weekly newspaper *The Colored American*, and a notable journalist. Born in Massachusetts, he had most of his career and life in New York City.

Born a free man in Falmouth, Massachusetts, Ray was the son of mail carrier Joseph Aspinwall Ray and his wife Annis Harrington. He attended Wesleyan Seminary in Wilbraham, Massachusetts, studying theology. In 1832 he enrolled as the first black student at Wesleyan University in Middletown, Connecticut, although his enrollment was revoked less than two months later. White students protested his admission

Katharine Lee Bates (August 12, 1859 – March 28, 1929) was an American professor and author, chiefly remembered for her anthem "America the Beautiful," but also for her many books and articles on social reform, on which she was a noted speaker.

The first draft of "America the Beautiful" was hastily jotted down in a notebook during the summer of 1893, which Bates spent teaching English at Colorado College in Colorado Springs, Colorado.

There is a statue of her on the lawn of Falmouth Library, and the library has an extensive collection of her works and memorabilia.

In the late 1800s, after railroad service was established between Boston and Cape Cod, **James Madison Beebe** bought over 700 acres and built Highfield Hall, which is now a museum, and St. Barnabas Church. Much of the land is preserved as Beebe Woods. James Madison Beebe made a fortune operating one of Boston's first department stores.

Robert Manry (June 2, 1918 – February 21, 1971) was a copy editor of the *Cleveland Plain Dealer* who in 1965 sailed from Falmouth, Massachusetts, to Falmouth, Cornwall, England, in a tiny 13.5-foot sailboat (an Old Town "Whitecap" built by the Old Town Canoe Co. of Old Town, Maine, which he had extensively modified for the voyage) named Tinkerbelle. Beginning on June 1, 1965, and ending on August 17, the voyage lasted 78 days.

An outdoor sculpture depicting the biologist, conservationist, and author, **Rachel Carson**, by David Lewis was installed in Waterfront Park in Woods Hole, on July 14, 2013. It was to mark the 50th anniversary of the publishing of Rachel Carson's book ***Silent Springs***, an environmental science book by Rachel Carson. The book was published on September 27, 1962, documenting the adverse environmental effects caused by the indiscriminate use of pesticides. Carson accused the chemical industry of spreading disinformation, and public officials of accepting the industry's marketing claims unquestioningly. The inscription on a plaque at the site of the sculpture reads:

"I had my first prolonged contact with the sea at Woods Hole. Never tired of watching the tidal currents pouring through the hole – that wonderful place of whirlpools and eddies and swiftly racing waters."

Do You Know – Falmouth?

Falmouth contains about 44 square miles, including 1,740 acres of freshwater ponds and about 1,500 acres of sheltered saltwater bays and harbors. Sixty-eight miles of seashore, 12 miles of which are sandy beaches, edge the town. The mean tidal range is from two to four feet along this coastline.

Falmouth was first recognized as an ideal summer resort by **Queen Awashonks** of the Narragansett tribes in Rhode Island, who is said to have spent several summers in what is now Falmouth Heights.

The town's first known settlers, the **Wampanoag** tribe, called it Suckanesset or "place by the sea where the black wampum is found." Valuable black wampum was made from quahog shells, always plentiful in Falmouth. The Wampanoags were the first to **cultivate cranberries** in Falmouth and the settlers continued the growing of cranberries.

Camp Edwards, formerly named Camp Falmouth, is a US military training camp in western Barnstable County. It is the largest part of Joint Base Cape Cod, formerly named Massachusetts Military Reservation.

Woods Hole is a strait in Massachusetts separating the Elizabeth Islands from the village of Woods Hole on the mainland of Cape Cod. It is one of four straits allowing maritime passage between Buzzards Bay and Vineyard Sound. The others are Canapitsit Channel, Robinson's Hole and Quick's Hole. Woods Hole is often referred to as **Woods Hole Passage** to distinguish it from the village of Woods Hole, which is itself named after the passage. The origin of the strait's name is unknown. Several similar straits in the area are also referred to as "holes," but this term is not used in the U.S. outside of the Cape and Islands

The Shining Sea Bikeway (SSB) was named for a line in the song *America the Beautiful*, written by Falmouth native Katharine Lee Bates. It follows the original route of the New York, New Haven and Hartford Railroad that used to run from Buzzards Bay, through North and West Falmouth, around Woods Hole and into Falmouth Station. In the early

1970s the Town of Falmouth purchased the right of way, tore up the tracks and officially opened the 3.3-mile Shining Sea Bikeway in 1975. In 2009, a new 7.4-mile section was added, extending the trail to North Falmouth.

It was with the opening of the railroad in 1872 that Falmouth began to develop as a **summer resort**. Wealthy men built imposing "cottages" on Penzance Point in Woods Hole, in Quissett, Sippewissett and Chapoquoit. Some of the summer residents became important benefactors to the town.

Located in the town of Falmouth, **Peterson Farm** is one of the oldest farms on Cape Cod. Its history began in 1679 and today visitors are invited to explore the fields and woodlands of this working sheep farm. The town of Falmouth eventually bought Peterson Farm in 1998 and sheep were brought back to the property, overseen by two shepherds. The town uses the sheep to mow down the fields and minimize the growth of invasive plants while bringing the farm back to its original purpose as a sheep farm.

The **Woods Hole Science Aquarium** is the oldest public aquarium in the country, established in 1885. Displaying over 140 animals from the greater Atlantic region, you can take a guided tour and watch daily feedings when the aquarium is open.

After the Allies began the invasion of North Africa in December 1942, the US Army built a prisoner-of-war camp for captured German soldiers in **Camp Edwards**. The camp, located at the south end of the runway, housed up to **2,000 POWs** at a given time, many of whom were from Rommel's famed Afrika Korps. The prisoners worked around Camp Edwards much of the time but were also sent to work in the area's farms and cranberry fields.

Cleveland East Ledge Light is a historic lighthouse in Falmouth. It sits on a man-made island in shallow water on the eastern of the two halves of Cleveland Ledge, which is said to have been named for President Grover Cleveland because he owned the nearby Gray Gables estate and used to fish in the area.

One of the Cape's most scenic hiking trails leads to **The Knob**, which is located in Woods Hole, Cornelia Carey Sanctuary. Take a hike along a sandy trail to a narrow slice of land where you can access the rocky outcropping that juts out into the water at the end. The view is spectacular. Many consider it one of the Cape's best secrets.

The Falmouth Playhouse (1949 to 1994) opened with Tallulah Bankhead doing the honors by smashing a bottle of champagne on a stage prop. In the following years, many top-notch actors came for the summer shows, including Helen Hayes, Sir Cedric Hardwicke, Joan Blondell, Lillian Gish, Eve Arden, Zasu Pitts, John Garfield, and Veronica Lake.

A treasure trove of **untold tales of Falmouth** can be found on YouTube.

All things cultural in Falmouth can be found at the **Museums on the Green** operated by the Falmouth Historical Society.

The **Crowell–Bourne Farm** is a historic 1775 farmhouse on West Falmouth Highway (Route 28A) in West Falmouth. The farm has been owned and operated by Salt Pond Areas Bird Sanctuaries since 1979. The property has 49 acres of fields and woods with walking trails, and is open to the public.

The first **Falmouth Road Race** in 1973 attracted 100 runners and now it attracts over 10,000 runners each year.

The **Barnstable County Fair** is a popular, family-friendly event that takes place at the Cape Cod Fairgrounds in East Falmouth. Every year families enjoy a week full of live music, magic displays, and livestock shows. The Barnstable County Fair has been a Cape Cod Tradition since 1844.

Crane Wildlife Management Area covers 1,883 acres of flat and rolling land in the inland village of Hatchville within the town of Falmouth in the southwestern part of Cape Cod. The WMA's land is mostly meadowland and coniferous forest on top of a dry, sandy surface.

The **Marine Biological Laboratory** (MBL) is an international center for research and education in biological and environmental science. Founded in Woods Hole in 1888, the MBL is a private, nonprofit institution affiliated with the University of Chicago. After being independent for most of its history, it became officially affiliated with the university on July 1, 2013. It also collaborates with numerous other institutions.

As of 2018, 58 Nobel Prize winners have been affiliated with **Marine Biological Laboratory** as students, faculty members or researchers. In addition, there are 280 members of the National Academy of Sciences and 236 Members of the American Academy of Arts and Sciences who have been affiliated with the lab.

Since **Old Silver Beach** in West Falmouth faces to the west, it is an excellent place to watch a sunset.

Nobska Light, originally called Nobsque Light, also known as **Nobska Point Light** is a lighthouse located near the division between Buzzards Bay, Nantucket Sound, and Vineyard Sound in the settlement of Woods Hole on the southwestern tip of Cape Cod. It overlooks Martha's Vineyard and Nonamesset Island. The light station was established in 1826, with the tower protruding above the keeper's house, and was replaced in 1876 by the current 42-foot-tall iron tower. It has been preserved and the adjoining house will become a maritime museum.

The Woods Hole Oceanographic Institution (WHOI, acronym pronounced /'huːi/ HOO-ee) is a private, nonprofit research and higher education facility dedicated to the study of marine science and engineering. Established in 1930 in Woods Hole, it is the largest independent oceanographic research institution in the U.S., with staff and students numbering about 1,000.

The Woods Hole Conference was held at Woods Hole as a response to the Soviet Union's launch of the Sputnik series of satellites, in 1959 to identify the problems of science education and to recommend solutions. Woods Hole Conference was held because American educators feared that the Soviet Union was surpassing the United States in educational emphasis on science, math, and foreign languages.

The conference marked the beginning of a new trend in educational planning: the unified efforts of distinguished people in varied fields addressing themselves to the general improvement of education. The result was discipline-based education and conceptual learning.

The **Church of the Messiah** in Woods Hole was built by Joseph Story Fay of Boston who bought up a great deal of land in Woods Hole and Falmouth. He is credited with having planted a variety of deciduous trees which has given Falmouth a different appearance from the rest of the Cape. The Fay Family gave Goodwill Park to the town.

The Town of Falmouth contains **eight villages**: Falmouth, East Falmouth, West Falmouth, North Falmouth, Hatchville, Teaticket, Waquoit, and Woods Hole. All but Hatchville have their own post office and four have elementary schools.

Joint Base Cape Cod (JBCC), adjacent to the towns of Falmouth, Mashpee, Bourne and Sandwich, employs hundreds of people. The Reservation includes the following facilities: Coast Guard Air Station Cape Cod, Upper Cape Regional Water Cooperative, Barnstable County Sheriff's Office, Otis National Guard, Mass. National Cemetery, Army National Guard Camp Edwards, Air Force Center for Engineering & the Environment, Sixth Missile Warning Squadron (PAVE PAWS), and U.S. Department of Agriculture, among others.

In 1960, the Massachusetts legislature created the **Woods Hole, Martha's Vineyard and Nantucket Steamship Authority** to provide for "adequate transportation of persons and necessaries of life for the Islands of Nantucket and Martha's Vineyard." This legislation empowered the Steamship Authority to acquire, maintain and operate a boat line between the mainland ports of Woods Hole (Falmouth) and Hyannis (Barnstable) and the Islands of Martha's Vineyard and Nantucket.

Many years of legal disputes followed **Historic Highfield**, as a group of citizens tried to stave off demolition and gain control of the building from its nonprofit owners. Volunteers cleared the lawn, boarded windows, and attempted to ward off further decay and vandalism. They also raised money and worked to convince residents that **Highfield Hall** was worth saving. Eventually, collaborating with local officials and politicians, Historic Highfield was able to convince the town that Highfield Hall was important to the community and extraordinary measures were warranted to save the property.

In 2000, Town Meeting Members authorized Falmouth Selectmen to take **Highfield Hall** and six acres by eminent domain, and in 2001 the Town signed a lease with Historic Highfield to renovate and operate Highfield Hall. The extraordinary restoration effort that followed was made possible through donations totaling more than $8,500,000 — almost all of which were contributed by private individuals.

Before the year 1870, what is now the **Falmouth Heights** area was known simply as the Great Hill. The area surrounding the Great Hill was largely untouched, save for the salt works that were found by the shore of Deacon's Pond.

All that changed when a group of Worcester businessmen happened upon the land after a visit to Martha's Vineyard. Their original plan for purchasing the land was to turn it into an A-list summer resort that would include cottages, hotels, stores and various means of transportation over the 100 acres of the Great Hill.

This is the original Falmouth Casino in Falmouth Heights. This building no longer exists; it was replaced by water-front condos and restaurant space.

"I was sitting in Arizona when I received Dogs on Cape Cod. Seeing the joy these dogs had playing on the beaches and in the marsh grasses on the Cape carried me back to my family visits in Harwich. The dogs are so full of life, it just made me smile."

Author: Betsy King

All About Harwich

Harwich (/ˈhɑːrwɪtʃ/ HAR-witch) is a New England town on Cape Cod, in Barnstable County. At the 2020 census it had a population of 13,440. The town is a popular vacation spot, located near the Cape Cod National Seashore. Harwich's beaches are on the Nantucket Sound side of Cape Cod. Harwich has three active harbors. Saquatucket, Wychmere and Allen Harbors are all in Harwich Port. The town of Harwich includes the villages of Pleasant Lake, West Harwich, East Harwich, Harwich Port, Harwich Center, North Harwich and South Harwich. Harwich was first settled by Europeans in 1670 as part of Yarmouth. The town was officially incorporated in 1694, and originally included the lands of the current town of Brewster. On September 14, 1994, the town celebrated its tricentennial, which marked 300 years since the town's founding on the same day in 1694.

John Wing appears to have been the first settler in this new territory in 1658 in what Brewster is now. In 1667, Indian Chief Sachemus gave John Mecoy a thirty-six acre parcel of land in what is now Harwich Center. Gershom Hall, the first white man to reside in Harwich, settled on this land in 1668. By 1694, there were enough settlers in the territory to support a minister, this being a requirement for application for incorporation by the General Court of the Massachusetts Bay Colony. This large tract of land, the largest in Barnstable County, remained intact until 1772 when the southeastern part was set off to Eastham.

Early industry involved fishing and farming. The town is considered by some to be the birthplace of the cranberry industry, with the first commercial operation opened in 1846. There are still many bogs in the town, although the economy is now more centered on tourism and as a residential community. The town is also the site of the start/finish line of the "Sail Around the Cape," which rounds the Cape counter-clockwise, returning via the Cape Cod Canal.

People of Significance – Harwich

Sidney Brooks was born in Harwich in 1813. He was educated at Phillips Academy in Andover, and went to Amherst College in Amherst, Massachusetts. After graduation, he taught at Chatham Academy. In 1843 he began plans to establish a private academy in Harwich. There was no public higher education beyond the elementary level in place at that time.

The school was to be built in a pine grove opposite the First Congregational Church. The architect for the project was Sidney's cousin, **Luther Gifford**. The plan was for a restrained and elegant Doric-style Greek revival building. After teaching all day in Chatham, Sidney worked, mostly by moonlight, laying out the grounds and walkways and selecting the trees to be removed.

The ceremony laying the cornerstone for **Pine Grove Seminary** was held August 3, 1844. In the cornerstone, under the northeast corner, was deposited a glass jar containing the names of the building committee, copies of Cape and Boston newspapers, and a list of the original subscribers. Subscribers each had bought shares in the school to finance its construction.

The Seminary opened December 14, 1844, with 45 students, mostly from Harwich. The two-room school was presided over by Sidney Brooks, and an assistant **Samuel Miller**. The school was open to men and women and offered courses typical of a high school curriculum at that time. The school year consisted of four quarters of 11 weeks each with two weeks of vacation between terms. Higher mathematics, at $4, including surveying and navigation, was the most expensive of the courses offered. English, French, Latin and Greek were also offered, as were piano and drawing. Students boarded with local families for $1.25 to $1.75 per week.

In the schoolroom there was a large blackboard at the south end, and blackboards filled the space between the windows on both sides. Compasses, quadrants, chronometers, surveyors' chains, and such were kept for student use. An opening in the south wall housed a sundial to aid navigation pupils in working out equations of time, etc.

Initially the building's exterior was white but was later repainted lilac with white trim. Many trees, flowers and shrubs were planted.

Anthony Elmer Crowell, also known as **A. Elmer Crowell** (December 5, 1862 – January 1, 1952) was a master decoy carver from East Harwich. Crowell specialized in shorebirds, waterfowl, and miniatures. Crowell's decoys are consistently regarded as the finest and most desirable decoys ever made.

Crowell's preening pintail drake and Canada goose decoys share the world record at $1.13 million dollars. Their private sales were orchestrated by Stephen O'Brien Jr. as part of what remains the largest decoy sale ever, with over thirty birds changing hands for approximately $7.5 million.

Crowell's barn/workshop was restored and moved to the grounds near the **Harwich Historical Society**. It is open to the public as a museum, commemorating his life and work.

Do You Know – Harwich

There are **three libraries** in Harwich. The municipal library, the **Brooks Free Library** in Harwich Center, is the largest and is a member of the Cape Libraries Automated Materials Sharing (CLAMS) library network. There are two smaller non-municipal libraries – the **Chase Library** on Route 28 in West Harwich at the Dennis town line, and the **Harwich Port Library** on Lower Bank Street in Harwich Port.

In 1927, during the addition of two rooms to the west side of Brooks Academy, the cornerstone was opened, and the contents of the time capsule were found to have turned to dust.

The **warm water** on the Nantucket Sound beaches located in Harwich is created by the position of Nantucket and Martha's Vineyard just south of its sunny beaches. That barrier protection and the shallower water leads to water temperatures that are much more comfortable for swimmers.

After the collapse of the fishing industry, Harwich turned its focus to the cultivation of what the Narragansett natives called the "bitter berry," or cranberry. Harwich can claim itself the birthplace of **commercial cranberry cultivation** in 1846. The crop continues to be the leading agricultural product of Massachusetts.

Bell's Neck Conservation lands are just north of the Platinum Pebble and offers spectacular views and convenient hiking and biking trails. One of the classic draws to the Cape are the cranberry bogs, some sit just north of Bell's Neck. The cultivation of the cranberry in the States started next door to Harwich in Dennis, in 1816.

The Lavender Farm is family-owned and located at the heart of eleven secluded acres. Our small farm boasts over 7,000 plants. The property is surrounded by seventy-five acres of conservation land with woodland walking trails. The farm is free to visit and open March-December. The lavender harvest occurs between late June to mid-July (peak bloom).

In August of 2015, the Harwich Junior Theatre officially changed its name to the **Cape Cod Theatre Company/Harwich Junior Theatre**. The change was significant in that it reflected the evolution of the organization from a small, seasonal venture to the pioneering force that it is today as a year-round center for theatre arts education and outreach – and a semi-professional theatre that mounts ten full-scale productions each year for audiences of more than 20,000. The new name intentionally maintains the reference to its significant Harwich Junior Theatre roots and history.

Harwich has the unique ability to provide **every form of aquatic activity available**: quiet canoeing through the great marshes of the Herring River, water skiing on Long Pond, deep sea fishing out of the harbors, fly fishing in several of the smaller ponds, or swimming and sunbathing on the sandy Nantucket Sound and Pleasant Bay beaches.

In 1803, after a bitter struggle, the north parish and south parish **separated** into the Towns of Brewster and Harwich.

When the whaling industry collapsed with the discovery of oil, the community's emphasis shifted to **cod fishing**. By 1802, 15 to 20 ships were shore fishing, and another four ships were cod fishing in Newfoundland and Labrador, and by 1851, there were forty-eight ships employing 577 men and bringing in thousands of tons of cod and mackerel. The eventual decline of the fishing industry in Harwich by the latter part of the 19th century was caused by increases in the size of ships which eventually outstripped the shallow port's ability to house them.

Over four hundred years ago, the Wampanoag Indians were the first to discover the pleasures of summering at **Wequassett**, swimming and fishing in the Bay's clear waters. They named the land Wequassett, which means "crescent on the water," because the sand-spit curves about the Cove are in the crescent shape. In 1665, Sachem John Quason Towsowett sold the land to William Nickerson, who eventually settled the town of Chatham.

The **Harwich Agricultural Commission** is the longest standing agricultural commission in Barnstable County and currently has seven members. Their goals include creating a stable permit application, hosting farmers' markets, and creating a right-to-farm bylaw.

The **Harwich Historical Society**, which seeks to preserve, collect, and interpret Harwich history through exhibitions, education programs, active collecting, and research, hosts a farmers market June through October at Brooks Academy Museum, 80 Parallel Street.

Harwich has many **different types of scenic landscapes**, which include; almost 11 miles of tidal shoreline along Nantucket Sound and Pleasant Bay; four harbors, where Round Cove is the only naturally occurring one and Wychmere, Allens, and Saquatucket were once pond and/or marsh areas, dredged out to the Sound to provide protection for sea vessels; many bogs which are scattered throughout Harwich providing scenic enjoyment and agricultural production; 22 freshwater ponds and two reservoirs; two scenic river corridors: Herring River and Muddy Creek; and over 320 acres of forests, water, and wetland in the Bells Neck Road/Salt Marsh/Reservoir area.

The eventual **decline of the fishing industry** in Harwich by the latter part of the 19th century was caused by increases in the size of ships which eventually outstripped the shallow port's ability to house them. Residents turned to the development of cranberry bogs and resorts for summer visitors, working side-by-side with Portuguese immigrants. The first resort hotel opened in 1880 and both the cranberry and the tourist industries remain substantial parts of Harwich's economy in the present.

There is **free parking** at the Tourism office on Main Street and Bank Street beach is a 9 minute walk or a 3 minute bike ride away. Save yourself the trouble of tight, crowded parking and a little money and be sure this is high on your list of hacks for Harwich.

Port Summer Nights take place Wednesday evenings in July and August on Main Street in Harwich Port. Bands, vendors, great shopping and food puts this at the top of our things to do in Harwich list.

There are 22 **freshwater swimming holes** on Cape Cod that are in the Town of Harwich. Almost all are pristine and great places to spend an afternoon. Some have easy access, like Long Pond, and others take a little bit of a hike to get to.

Reed Books in Harwich Port has a book selection that is extensive, both used and new. It has great prices on new books. Clean space, kind owners, and a great selection. The owners and staff offer kind and courteous service. A must visit bookstore in Harwich Port.

All About Mashpee

Mashpee /ˈmæʃpi/ is a town in Barnstable County. The population was 15,060 as of 2020. The town is the site of the headquarters and most members of the Mashpee Wampanoag Tribe, one of two federally recognized Wampanoag groups.

After English colonists arrived, they began to settle the area of present-day Mashpee in 1658 with the assistance of the missionary Richard Bourne, from the neighboring town of Sandwich. In 1660 the colonists allowed those Christian Wampanoag who had been converted about fifty square miles in the English settlement. Beginning in 1665, the Wampanoag governed themselves with a court of law and trials according to English custom (they had long governed themselves according to their own customs).

The "Old Indian Meeting House," built in 1684 at Mashpee, is the oldest Native American church in the United States.

Following their defeat in King Philip's War (1675–1676), the Wampanoag of the mainland were resettled with the Sakonnet in present-day Rhode Island. Others of the people were brought, together with the Nauset, into the praying towns, such as Mashpee, in Barnstable County. There were also Wampanoag on Martha's Vineyard and other areas.

The colonists designated Mashpee on Cape Cod as the largest Indian reservation in Massachusetts. The town's name is an Anglicization of a native name, mass-nippe: mass is "great", or "greater" (see Massachusetts), and nippe is "water." The name has been translated as "the greater cove" or "great pond," or "land near great cove," where the water being referenced is Wakeby Pond, which is greater at one end.

In the year 1763, the British Crown designated Mashpee as a plantation, against the will of the Wampanoag. Designation as a plantation meant that the area governed by the Mashpee Wampanoag was integrated into the colonial district of Mashpee. The colony gave the natives the "right" to elect their own officials to maintain order in their area, but otherwise subjected them to colonial government. The population of the plantation declined steadily due to the conditions placed upon the Wampanoag. They also suffered from encroachment on their lands by the English.

Following the American Revolutionary War, the town in 1788 revoked Mashpee self-government, which European-American officials considered a failure. They appointed a committee, consisting of five European-American members, to supervise the Mashpee. William Apess, a Pequot Methodist preacher, helped the Mashpee Wampanoag lead a peaceful protest of this action, and the governor threatened a military response.

In 1834, the state returned a certain level of self-government to the Wampanoag, although they were not completely autonomous. With the idea that emulating European-American farming would encourage assimilation, in 1842 the state broke up some of the Wampanoag communal land. It distributed 2,000 acres of their 13,000-acre property in allotments of 60-acre parcels to heads of households, so that each family could have individual ownership for subsistence farming.

The legislature passed laws against the encroachments on Wampanoag land by European Americans but did not enforce them. The competing settlers also stole wood from the reservation. It was a large region, once rich in wood, fish, and game, and desired by white settlers, who envied the growing community of Mashpee. The Mashpee Indians suffered more conflicts with their white neighbors than did other more isolated or less desirable Indigenous settlements in the state.

In 1870, the state approved the incorporation of Mashpee as a town, the second-to-last jurisdiction on the Cape to undergo the process. Ultimately the Wampanoag lost control of their land and self-government. Many of their descendants have remained in the area and identified as Mashpee by their communal culture.

In the early 1970s, the Mashpee tribe reorganized and filed a land claim against the state for the loss of lands. While they did not win their case, the Mashpee continued to develop as an organized community and gained federal recognition as a tribe in 2007.

Today the town of Mashpee is known both for tourist recreation and for its distinctive minority Wampanoag culture. The population is predominately European American in ancestry. As the town attracts numerous summer visitors, there are many seasonal businesses and service jobs to support this tourism.

The Mashpee Wampanoag Tribe has its headquarters here. In 2015 the Department of Interior evaluated taking into trust 170 acres in Mashpee as a reservation for the Wampanoag, who already controlled the land, however in 2018 the request was rejected. This decision also applied to the 150 acres in Taunton, Massachusetts, which the Wampanoag tribe had acquired.

That action was challenged in October 2016 by a United States District Court decision, reached after a suit was filed earlier that year by opponents to Mashpee Wampanoag plans to build a gaming casino on their Taunton land.

The Wampanoag hold an annual pow-wow at which they display both modern and traditional activities and crafts.

People of Significance – Mashpee

Samuel Gross Davis was a benefactor of the school children of Mashpee. He was a wealthy resident of Boston. He left 10 percent of his estate because as his will reads "...by family tradition one of my ancestors was an Indian woman of Concord, Massachusetts, and as the inhabitants of Mashpee which is near beautiful West Falmouth are mostly Indians and negroes." Mashpee requested and received permission from the Probate Court to use some of these funds to construct a new school in 1939, which bears the name Samuel G. Davis. Mashpee schools continue to benefit from the estate.

William Apess (1798–1839, Pequot), was an ordained Methodist minister, writer, and activist of mixed-race descent, who was a political and religious leader in Massachusetts. After becoming ordained as a Methodist minister in 1829, he published his autobiography the same year. It is among the first autobiographies by a Native American writer. Apess was part Pequot by descent, especially through his mother's family, and identified with their culture.

In 1833, while serving as an itinerant preacher in New England, Apess visited the Mashpee on Cape Cod. Hearing their grievances against white overseers and settlers who stole their wood, he helped organize what was called the Mashpee Revolt of 1833-34. Their attempt to regain civil rights was covered sympathetically by the *Boston Advocate* but criticized by local journals on Cape Cod. Apess published a book about the experience in 1835, which he summarized as "Indian Nullification."

Apess has been described as "perhaps the most successful activist on behalf of Native American rights in the antebellum United States."

Prior to 1870, **land in Mashpee** could only to be sold to other proprietors of Mashpee. After 1870 with restrictions removed, land was sold to speculators and cranberry growers.

Only a few residents remained in South Mashpee during the early 1900s, when land accumulators and speculators, such as The Greater Cotuit Shore Company, established in 1917, purchased much of the acreage on Mashpee's shores – the beaches, bluffs, and fields known today as Popponesset and New Seabury. Beginning in 1929, **Malcolm G. Chace**, an industrialist from Rhode Island, and fellow associates of Nantucket Sound Associates bought the lands of Greater Cotuit Shore Company, as well as that of the cranberry growers, and residents. Chace created new businesses – Popponesset Beach, Inc., Popponesset Corporation, Realty Operators, Fields Point Manufacturing Company, and finally the New Seabury Corporation.

Chace's sons, Malcolm G., Jr., and Arnold B. "Buff" are credited with the creation of New Seabury. In 1960 the Chaces hired William Warner to design New Seabury and Emil Hanslin to develop the seaside community. Bright Coves was the first of several villages to open, and its four model homes were featured in *Life* and *American Home* magazines in 1962. A small ferry serviced prospective purchasers. Highwood Village, catering to equestrians, opened in 1964 with ninety-one home sites. That same year, the clubhouse, and Championship Golf Course and nine holes of the Executive Course were completed (the remaining nine holes opened in 1965).

Because of two lawsuits, construction at New Seabury was halted between 1971 and 1977 and another suit was filed in 1977 but settled in 1979, when construction was resumed.

Crispus Attucks (c.1723 – March 5, 1770) was an American whaler, sailor, and stevedore of African and Native American descent, generally regarded as the first person killed in the Boston Massacre and thus the first American killed in the American Revolution. Historians disagree on whether he was a free man or an escaped slave, but most agree that he was of Native American (specifically Wampanoag) and African descent.

Do You Know – Mashpee?

The **Town Barn** located on Route 130 was Mashpee's first Town Hall.

Market Street Book Shop is an independent bookstore in Mashpee commons. The owner and staff are known for their knowledge of books and their customer friendly service. You will surely find the book you are seeking among their well-stocked book shelves.

Mashpee's first library was housed in the Public Hall Library Society building in the 1890s, and later in the North Mashpee School. In 1928, $1,625 was appropriated for a library building. That building is pictured in 1961 when it was moved north a few hundred yards while the addition to Davis school was completed. The building was sold and the library operated for three years in the cafeteria of the school.

In 1831the Legislature voted $400 for **two schools** in Mashpee in 1831. The South Mashpee School was built in 1831 at the southwest corner of today's Great Oak and Red Brook roads. It was used as a school until 1900, and it was purchased the next year by the Young People's Baptist Society and used for religious services. Sold to Fields Point Mfg. Co. in 1953, it was donated by the New Seabury Company to the Town in 1975 as part of the Bicentennial celebration and moved to its present location next to the Meeting House.

In 1934, Norma Armstrong on the land, known as the **Popponesset shores**, operated as a tourist camp and small store. An article in the May 3, 1940, *Enterprise* describes sixteen cottages already completed at Popponesset and a restaurant with "...large mullioned windows offering a view of the sea in all directions" (today's Popponesset Inn).

Mashpee Wampanoag Indian Museum is a cultural center in the town of Mashpee. The museum ground itself is well known for the Avant House as well as hosting the Mill Pond Herring Ladder, a Fish ladder on the Mashpee River. The museum was established in 1997 through a town meeting vote. Since 1999 the site has been listed under the National Register of Historic Places.

The Cape Cod Children's Museum, in Mashpee, is a place where families and children can learn and play together.

The museum features lots of hand-on exhibits to discover and explore, such as, the Pirate Ship, and visitors can see the stars at the indoor planetarium, or create their own stories at the Puppet Theatre.

South Cape Beach State Park is a state park located in the town of Mashpee. It is part of the Waquoit Bay National Estuarine Research Reserve. The park is situated between Waquoit Bay and Vineyard Sound and features barrier beach and dunes, salt marsh, scrub oak and pitch pine woodland and kettle ponds and is managed by the Department of Conservation and Recreation. The park has a 1-mile (1.6 km) white sand beach that is handicap-accessible with handicap-accessible restrooms. Facilities for hiking and walking include over-the-dune boardwalks and scenic viewing areas.

The history and culture of the Wampanoag from the Stone Age to the present is carefully detailed through a range of exhibits at the **Mashpee Wampanoag Museum**. First established under the guidance of the Mashpee Historical Commission, the Museum is the only one in existence devoted exclusively to Wampanoag history. Displays include a variety of tools, baskets, hunting and fishing implements, weapons, and domestic utensils. The focal point in the exhibits is a large diorama depicting a typical scene from an early Wampanoag settlement.

Camp Edwards was the home to German POWs during World War II. There were as many as two thousand German prisoners at one time. There was even a mock German village constructed for training. The prisoners worked various jobs around the base and were also sent to work on nearby farms and in local cranberry bogs.

Otis Air National Guard Base is named for pilot, flight surgeon, and eminent Boston City Hospital surgeon Lt. Frank "Jesse" Otis. He was a member of the 101st Observation Squadron who was killed on January 11, 1937, when his Douglas O-46A crashed at Hennepin, Illinois, while on a cross-country training mission.

On September 11, 2001, the North American Aerospace Defense Command alerted the base at 8:41 to be put on battle stations. Four minutes later, Lieutenant Colonel Timothy Duffy and Major Daniel Nash were scrambled and flew F-15 Eagle fighters out of the base heading toward New York City to intercept American Airlines Flight 11. They departed somewhere between 8:46 and 8:52.

Mashpee's Wampanoag roots are ever-present in the **Old Indian Meeting House**, which remains the oldest church on Cape Cod and the oldest Native American church in the United States. Built in 1684, it is now on the National Register of Historic Places.

Mashpee National Wildlife Refuge is in the towns of Mashpee and Falmouth, with six thousand acres, it is the Cape's second largest open, accessible conservation land, behind only the National Seashore. It was named after the Mashpee Wampanoag Tribe, "the people of the first light." It is unique within the National Wildlife Refuge System in that it is the only refuge that is managed cooperatively by eight conservation landowners and the Friends organization: a consortium of federal, state, tribal, private and nonprofit. It is the model for future refuges.

On May 21, 1833, the **Mashpees** agreed to tell Massachusetts Governor Levi Lincoln that "we, as a tribe, will rule ourselves, and have a right to do so; for all men are born free and equal." This was the opening salvo in the Mashpee revolt of 1833.

Between 1846 and 2008, the shoreline of South Cape Beach has been retreating landward at an average rate of 1.4 feet per year. Continued acceleration in the rate of sea level rise, coupled with an increase in the intensity and frequency of extreme storms will likely lead to an increased rate of land loss. Local losses may be greater than those predicted.

The **Mashpee Pine Barrens** are an important ecosystem on the Cape as they are home to the New England Cottontail, a species that is of concern. The dense shrub oak found on the parcel provides ideal habitat for this rabbit. In order to preserve the vital habitat, this parcel has been burned to remove overgrowth, such as pitch pines, that reduces the amount of low growing scrub oak.

All About Orleans

Orleans (/ɔːrˈliːnz/ or-LEENZ) is a town in Barnstable County. The population was 6,307 at the 2020 census.

Orleans was first settled in 1693 by Pilgrims from the Plymouth Colony who were dissatisfied with the poor soil and small tracts of land granted to them. Originally the southern parish of neighboring Eastham, Orleans was officially incorporated in 1797. Orleans was named in honor of Louis Philippe II, Duke of Orléans, in recognition of France's support for the 13 colonies during the American Revolution, and because the town did not want an English name, as they had been captured twice by the British during the war.

Early history, like much of the Cape, revolved around fishing, whaling and agriculture. As the fishing industry grew, salt works sprang up in the town to help preserve the catches. However, the town's growth helped deplete the town of lumber, a situation that did not begin to be remedied until the railroad came and brought lumber from the mainland in the mid-to-late 19th century. The rail also helped bring tourism to the town. In 1898, the French Cable Company built a 3,200-mile-long (5,100 km) transatlantic cable to Orleans, which operated from the French Cable Station. The town's historical society is in the 1834 Universalist Meeting House.

People of Significance – Orleans

Only **Nicholas Snow**, who established his homestead at Namskaket, was on the Orleans side of the division line of 1797. Nicholas Snow arrived in Plymouth on the Ann in 1623, and married Constance Hopkins, daughter of Mayflower passenger Stephen Hopkins. After relocating to Nauset/Eastham, he held the positions of surveyor, deputy, tax collector, constable, and selectman while there. He died in 1676, well before the separation, but can Orleans claim him as their honorary first citizen?

John Kendrick was born in 1740 in what was then part of the Town of Harwich (now Orleans) on Cape Cod. He was an American sea captain during the American Revolutionary War, and was involved in the exploration and maritime fur trading of the Pacific Northwest alongside his subordinate Robert Gray. He was the leader of the first US expedition to the Pacific Northwest. He is known for his role in the 1789 Nootka Crisis, having been present at Nootka Sound when the Spanish naval officer José Esteban Martínez seized several British ships belonging to a commercial enterprise owned by a partnership of companies under John Meares and Richard Cadman Etches. This incident nearly led to war between Britain and Spain and became the subject of lengthy investigations and diplomatic inquiries.

Kendrick was the first American to try to open trade with Japan. He began the Hawaiian sandalwood trade. He was killed during an exchange of cannon salutes with the ship Jackal when one of the cannons was loaded, purportedly by accident. John Kendrick was instrumental in pioneering trade in the Pacific Northwest, the Hawaiian Islands, and China, as well as helping the young United States establish itself as global trade power.

Originally known as South Parish of Eastham, which was settled in 1644, Orleans became incorporated in 1797 after seeking independence since 1717. The **Nauset Indians** were the native people of the area. The relationship between the settlers and native Americans was peaceful and co-operative. The present Nauset Heights area was the farming site of the Indigenous people. The last of their settlements lived in South Orleans.

Sea Captains and ordinary seamen of Orleans manned the merchant and whaling vessels during the age of sail. The sea has influenced the economy of Orleans from the beginning to the present. Salt works were located on the bay and Town cove shores. There were many domestic needs for salt and the fishing fleet's requirements were large for fish preservation. Finally with the discovery of salt deposits in the U.S. the salt-making industry became obsolete in the 1850s.

> "The Pilgrims landed the Mayflower at Cape Cod, Massachusetts, on a cold November day in 1620 because they were running out of beer."
>
> Author: Susan Cheever

Do You Know – Orleans?

On July 21, 1918, the tiny town of Orleans (population 1,012 at the time) was **shelled by a German U-boat** making it the only point on U.S. soil attacked during World War I. The German submarine, U-156 attacked the tug Perth Amboy, heading south about three miles off Nauset Beach with four barges in tow.

The **Cable Station Museum** commemorates part of American History. During World War I, General Pershing in France communicated with the US Government through this cable station. In 1927, the message that Charles Lindbergh had landed in Paris came through this station from Paris. It was then sent to the rest of the United States.

The Chocolate Sparrow opened as a simple candy shop in 1989 in North Eastham. Gradually they learned the art of making fine chocolate and the business of selling it. In 1991 they opened a summer shop in Wellfleet. Two years later in Orleans, they opened The Hot Chocolate Sparrow, a cafe complete with coffee from around the world, desserts of every indulgence, and their own hand-dipped chocolates. Here they could offer specialty coffee drinks in a sophisticated but welcoming atmosphere. It has grown into a local institution, open early morning to late night, every day of the year except Christmas.

The **Academy of Performing Arts**, originally known as The Orleans Arena Theater, was founded by Betsy (born 1922) and Gordon Argo (born 1924) in 1950 for performing summer stock theater in the round. The couple's three children, Allison, Elizabeth, and Walter grew up around the theater and helped their parents run it. The children also acted in some of the theater's productions. Kurt Vonnegut, Jr. wrote a play, Penelope, which was performed at the theater. Penelope later became Happy Birthday, Wanda June, a feature film released in 1971. By 1976 the Argos had long since divorced and for assorted reasons the theater was sold by Mrs. Argo.

So, You Think You Know Cape Cod?

The Centers for Culture and History in Orleans is housed in a Greek Revival building that is on the National Register of Historic Places. It was formerly used as the Meeting House for the Universalist Church of Orleans.

One of these exhibits is of the **lifesaving tradition** on the Cape. This legacy dates back almost 170 years before Orleans was incorporated as a separate municipality. During the winter of 1626-1627, the Sparrowhawk was wrecked off the shores of what became Orleans, and the first documented rescue mission was headed by none other than Governor William Bradford of Plymouth Colony.

The **Motor Lifeboat CG36500** is nothing short of a floating museum. Built in 1946, she performed admirably during her years of service at the Chatham Lifeboat Station. On an incredible night on the high seas off Chatham back in 1952, the Coast Guard craft rescued the Pendleton and most of its crew. The story is now a major motion picture and book, *The Finest Hours*. The boat is docked at Rock Harbor, Orleans, during the summer months for public viewing.

It was in 1814 that the **Battle of Rock Harbor** took place in the vicinity of the titular harbor. Though not by any means a major battle of the War of 1812,

Rock Harbor is located at the point on Cape Cod where the shoreline begins to drift northward.

Wagon tracks and horseshoe prints have emerged in several broad strips at the water's edge on Nauset Beach. They date back to the late 18th or early 20th century.

"JS 1660" are the oldest initials, the imprint of **Jonathan Sparrow**, who in the 1600s received a land grant here of one hundred acres from the King of England. For two hundred years, Sparrow and his descendants tilled and toiled in these wind-swept meadows rolling down to Mill Pond, Robert's Cove, and the ocean beyond breaking on Nauset Beach. In the 1800s, Captain Benjamin Sparrow (1839-1906) built the spacious colonial perched like a clipper ship on a hill shaded by huge elms.

Water power was first used to turn millstones to grind grain but with the shortage of fast running rivers and streams, Cape Codders turned to the wind for power. **Jonathan Young Windmill** was built in the early

1700s in South Orleans. By 1839 it was moved to overlook the Town Cove on the present hillside site of The Governor Prence Motor Inn on Rte. 6A. During the recent restoration it was relocated to the small park on the shore of Town Cove where it stands today.

Sea Howl Bookshop offers a thoughtfully curated selection of new books of all genres, along with a smaller number of used, vintage and out-of-print titles, and periodicals. In addition to reading materials, the shop carries stock paper goods for the discerning writer and pen pal - including greeting cards, stationery, and journals - and puzzles and games to keep brains happy. There is in-store and online shopping, with curbside pickup and shipping options.

In 1658 the son of a Mayflower Pilgrim purchased what became **Deacon Rogers Meadow** from the Nauset Indians, to obtain a source of vital salt hay, as winter fodder for cattle. Now the marsh is considered critical for the health and preservation of Pleasant Bay. The acreage has been added to and now has been donated to the Orleans Conservation Trust.

The **Community of Jesus** is a charismatic monastic Christian community which is located near Rock Harbor.

Today according to the group, approximately 225 professed members, together with another fifty children and young people live as households in thirty privately owned, multifamily homes that surround the church and the guesthouse. This also includes the twenty-five celibate brothers who are living in the "Zion Friary" and the sixty celibate sisters who are living in the "Bethany Convent." Altogether, the Community of Jesus consists of almost 275 people, from many walks of life and various church backgrounds - including Presbyterian, Episcopalian, Congregational, Baptist, Lutheran, Anglican, Methodist, Pentecostal, and Roman Catholic.

All About Provincetown

Provincetown /ˈprɒvɪnsˌtaʊn/ is a New England town located at the extreme tip of Cape Cod in Barnstable County. A small coastal resort town with a year-round population of 3,664 as of the 2020 United States Census, Provincetown has a summer population as high as 60,000. Often called "P-town" or "P'town," the locale is known for its beaches, harbor, artists, tourist industry, and as a popular vacation destination for the LGBT+ community.

At the time of European encounter, the area was long settled by the historic Nauset tribe, who had a settlement known as "Meeshawn." They spoke Massachusett, a Southern New England Algonquian language dialect that they shared in common with their closely related neighbors, the Wampanoag.

On May 15, 1602, having made landfall from the west and believing it to be an island, Bartholomew Gosnold initially named this area "Shoal Hope." Later that day, after catching a "great store of codfish," he chose instead to name this outermost tip of land "Cape Cod." Notably, that name referred specifically to the area of modern-day Provincetown; it wasn't until much later that that name was reused to designate the entire region now known as Cape Cod.

On November 9, 1620, the Pilgrims aboard the *Mayflower* sighted Cape Cod while en route to the Colony of Virginia. After two days of failed attempts to sail south against the strong winter seas, they returned to the safety of the harbor, known today as Provincetown Harbor, and set anchor. It was here that the Mayflower Compact was drawn up and signed. They agreed to settle and build a self-governing community and came ashore in the West End.

Though the Pilgrims chose to settle across the bay in Plymouth, Cape Cod enjoyed an early reputation for its valuable fishing grounds and for its harbor. In 1654, the Governor of the Plymouth Colony purchased this land from the Chief of the Nausets, for a selling price of two brass kettles, six coats, 12 hoes, 12 axes, 12 knives and a box.

That land, which spanned from East Harbor (formerly, Pilgrim Lake) near the present-day border between Provincetown and Truro to Long Point, was kept for the benefit of Plymouth Colony, which began leasing fishing rights to roving fishermen. In 1678, the fishing grounds were opened up to allow the inclusion of fishermen from the Massachusetts Bay Colony.

In 1692, a new Royal Charter combined the Plymouth and Massachusetts Bay colonies into the Province of Massachusetts Bay. "Cape Cod" was thus officially renamed the "Province Lands."

The first record of a municipal government with jurisdiction over the Province Lands was in 1714, with an Act that declared it the "Precinct of Cape Cod," annexed under control of Truro.

The Massachusetts General Court named the Precinct of Cape Cod as a new township Provincetown in 1727.

In 1893, the Massachusetts General Court changed the Town's charter, giving the townspeople deeds to the properties they held, while still reserving unoccupied areas.

The population of Provincetown remained small through most of the 18th century.

The town was affected by the American Revolution the same way most of Cape Cod was: the effective British blockade shut down most fish production and shipping and the town dwindled.

Following the American Revolution, Provincetown grew rapidly as a fishing and whaling center. The population was bolstered by numerous Portuguese sailors, many of whom were from the Azores, and settled in Provincetown after being hired to work on US ships.

By the 1890s, Provincetown was booming and began to develop a resident population of writers and artists, as well as a summer tourist industry. After the 1898 Portland Gale severely damaged the town's fishing industry, members of the town's art community took over many of the abandoned buildings. By the early decades of the 20th century, the town had acquired an international reputation for its artistic and literary productions.

Its **origins as a mecca for the LGBT+ community** lie with the arrival of Tennessee Williams in 1940. He joined a group "dominated by a platinum blonde Hollywood belle named Doug and a bull-dike named Wanda who [was] a well-known writer under a male pen name." Ptown, he wrote, was "screaming with creatures not all of whom are seagulls." Other factors were its remoteness and the Portuguese homeowners who rented rooms in their home for low prices and the art studio Charles Webster Hawthorne started in 1899 called the Cape Cod School of Art. These factors led to the arrival of free thinkers from Greenwich Village.

In 1952, Provincetown selectmen enacted regulations that banned drag shows and forbade bars and restaurants from encouraging "the habitual gathering place for homosexuals of either sex." "Selectmen Clamp Down on Gay Spots with New Regulations to Curb Evils," reported the *Provincetown Advocate* in 1952. The regulations failed to curb any evils.

The battle continued until the **"Shopkeepers Plea,"** saying Provincetown was no longer a comfortable vacation spot and was become less interesting and less entertaining. The shopkeepers won.

> "One of my favorite vacation memories was the Thai foot massage and Internet access salons in Bangkok, followed up by my testing cellphone coverage while wading in Provincetown Harbor on Cape Cod."
>
> Author: Kara Swisher

People of Significance – Provincetown

On May 15, 1602, having made landfall from the west and believing it to be an island, **Bartholomew Gosnold** initially named this area "Shoal Hope." Later that day, after catching a "great store of codfish", he chose instead to name this outermost tip of land "Cape Cod. Notably, that name referred specifically to the area of modern-day Provincetown; it wasn't until much later that that name was reused to designate the entire region now known as Cape Cod.

In 1899 **Charles Webster Hawthorne** opened the Cape Cod School of Art, said to be the first outdoor school for figure painting, in Provincetown. Film of his class from 1916 has been preserved.

The playwright **Tennessee Williams**, then twenty-nine, arrived in the summer of 1940. He joined a group "dominated by a platinum blonde Hollywood belle named Doug and a bull-dike named Wanda who [was] a well-known writer under a male pen name." Ptown, he wrote, was "screaming with creatures not all of whom are seagulls."

Provincetown is often cited as a birthplace of American theater. It is where our first internationally renowned playwright **Eugene O'Neill** crafted some of his earliest masterpieces with the Provincetown Players.

Marsden Hartley called it "the Great Summer of 1916." Many artists, like Hartley, had recently returned to America from Berlin, Paris, and London because of World War I. They had experienced the relaxed attitudes toward sex in those cities, and they liked it.

The artists flocked to Provincetown, which that year had six art schools. *The Boston Globe* ran a page one story headlined, "Biggest Art Colony in the World in Provincetown."

Norman Mailer used to summer in Provincetown. His will stipulated that his home be transformed into a writer's colony, which it has.

There are many well-known names and less well-known names that have contributed to the Provincetown of today.

Best description comes from the Provincetown office of Tourism:

"Provincetown has long been connected to a sense of freedom, from the Pilgrims' first landing on its shores to the Town's enduring appeal for gay and lesbian travelers. Over the years, an eclectic mix of fishermen, whalers, artists, writers, Catholic Portuguese immigrants, and members of the LGBTQ+ community have called it home. Today, seasoned visitors and newcomers alike are still drawn to this sandy tip of the cape for its beauty, its color, and its sheer flamboyance."

The Mayflower Compact Monument commemorates the Mayflower Pilgrims' first landing in the New World in Provincetown. The compact was to ensure a degree of law and order in this place where they had not been granted a patent to settle. Myles Standish was one of the 41 men who signed it in Provincetown harbor.

Do You Know – Provincetown?

The unique, green-grey exterior of the **Provincetown Town Hall** foretells the inside of the historic building is even more spectacular. On the second floor is a magnificent hall that is also a venue for shows and events throughout the summer.

Provincetown's **year-round population** reached its zenith in 1875, with 4,357 people – slightly more than today. By 1885, the town had fifty-five wharves and 114 schooners.

In the early **1700s Provincetown** was a transient, seasonal community, described as a wild place inhabited by "fishermen, smugglers, outlaws, escaped indentured servants, heavy drinkers and the 'Mooncussers.'"

The Provincetown Players was an important experimental theatre company formed during this period. Many of its members lived during other parts of the year in Greenwich Village in New York, and intellectual and artistic connections were woven between the places.

In 1898 Charles Webster Hawthorne opened the **Cape Cod School of Art**, said to be the first outdoor school for figure painting, in Provincetown. Film of his class from 1916 has been preserved. The school exists today as the **Cape School of Art**, offering workshops, classes and lectures to inform a new generation of artists and patrons.

The **Fine Arts Work Center**, founded in 1968, is a leading long-term residency program for emerging artists and writers and one of the world's most renowned.

Whale watching as a science and tourist attraction started in Provincetown in 1975 when scientist Stormy Mayo from the Provincetown Center for Coastal Studies teamed up with charter fishing boat Captain Al Avellar to observe and study the three species of whales that are found in the waters around Provincetown: the fin, humpback, and right whale.

The Cape Cod Pilgrim Memorial Association, Cape Cod's oldest not-for-profit organization, built the **Pilgrim Monument** to commemorate the Mayflower Pilgrims' first landing in the New World in Provincetown, in November 1620. President Theodore Roosevelt laid the cornerstone in 1907. In 1910, President William Howard Taft dedicated the finished 252-foot, 7 and ½ inch tower, and it is the tallest all-granite structure in the United States.

The town includes eight buildings and two historic districts on the **National Register of Historic Places**: Provincetown Historic District and Dune Shacks of Peaked Hill Bars Historic District.

In the mid-1960s, Provincetown saw population growth. The town's rural character appealed to the **hippies of the era**; property was relatively cheap and rents were correspondingly low, especially during the winter. Many of those who came stayed and raised families. Commercial Street, the town's "Main Street," gained numerous cafés, leather shops, head shops – various hip small businesses blossomed and many flourished.

By the 1970s, Provincetown had a significant **gay population**, especially during the summer tourist season, when restaurants, bars and small shops serving the tourist trade were open. There had been a gay presence in Provincetown as early as the start of the 20th century as the artists' colony developed, along with experimental theatre. Drag queens could be seen in performance as early as the 1940s in Provincetown.

In 1978 the **Provincetown Business Guild** (PBG) was formed to promote gay tourism. More than 200 businesses belong to the PBG, and Provincetown is the best-known gay summer resort on the East Coast.

The 2010 US Census revealed Provincetown to have the highest rate of **same-sex couples** in the US, at 163.1 per one thousand households.

Bear Week is the largest gathering of bears in the world. Tens of thousands come to Provincetown during this annual event to go to parties, bars, and clubs throughout the town. You know what you are getting into when you attend.

Fantasia Fair is a week-long transgender event held every October in Provincetown. The first Fair was held in 1975 which makes Fantasia Fair the longest-running transgender event in the world. It has been and continues to be a model for other transgender conferences.

Single Women's Weekend is for all those looking for love. With special events like speed dating, dance parties, mixers, and more, this weekend is the perfect time to find that special someone.

The Provincetown Portuguese Festival celebrates the Portuguese culture and heritage in Provincetown. It includes a blessing of the fleet.

In 2017, a memorial was dedicated to those who lost their lives to AIDS. The **Provincetown AIDS Memorial** is located at Provincetown Town Hall on the lawn at the Ryder Street entrance. The Memorial has been sculpted from 16.5 tons of carbon gray Quartzite, a stone strong enough to stand up through the freezing and thawing of New England winters and constant salt air. The stone was sculpted in Tuscany with the aid of CNC robotic stone milling equipment and then finished by hand.

There is nothing like an LGBTQ+ event to make Provincetown's streets teem from coast to coast. Celebrations like **Carnival** in August attract some 90,000 people, especially for the flamboyant parade down Commercial Street. In Provincetown, gay and lesbian events go all summer long.

Provincetown was ranked the **most bikeable small city** in the nation by the PeopleForBikes organization in 2021. Not only that, but P-Town was also ranked the fourth most bikeable small city in the world by the same organization.

AAA recently made it official by declaring **Race Point Beach** one of the five best beaches in New England. Race Point Beach was the only beach on Cape Cod, or in Massachusetts for that matter, to earn a spot on the list.

Province Lands Bike Trail in Provincetown cannot be beat. Next time you are looking to go on a bike ride with beautiful views of the Cape Cod coast and the amazing sand dunes upon it, take the Province Lands Bike Trail. It is 6.6 miles long.

Provincetown's **Long Point Lighthouse** may sit in one of the Cape's most remote locations, but more than 200 years ago it was home to a thriving village. Found on the extreme tip of Cape Cod, the hidden village of Long Point was a popular spot for fishermen. Remoteness and time spelled the death of the village. Today there are no residents.

Race Point Lighthouse, built in 1876, is known by its white tower showing a flashing white light every 10 seconds, visible for 16 nautical miles. Visitors may enjoy memorable day trips and even overnight stays.

In the 1920s is when Provincetown first emerged as an **artist's colony**. Today, Provincetown is still considered the oldest continuous art colony in the nation.

At least three and possibly four houses in Provincetown were used as stops on the **Under Ground Railroad**, because in a sense, we do have a border with Canada: The Atlantic Ocean. Cape Cod fishermen would take escaping slaves out to sea at night to meet Canadian fishermen off the coasts of Nova Scotia and Newfoundland, to bring them to safety.

The Provincetown Art Association and Museum (PAAM) is accredited by the American Alliance of Museums and is the most attended art museum on Cape Cod. The museum's permanent collection includes over 2,500 objects, a number which continues to grow through donations and new acquisitions. PAAM mounts approximately forty exhibitions each year.

As **Dune Shacks Trail** is a hike completely on sand, you will want to make sure to wear proper shoes or it may be difficult to obtain traction.

The **lobster industry** in North America started here, and Provincetown was the first lobster center of New England. In 1740, large Provincetown lobsters were selling in Boston for three half-pence apiece! But the industry really got going around 1800.

Before the railroad, **getting to Provincetown** was on a road, The King's Highway, that was laid out around the sand dunes of the Eastern Harbor, over a track in the sand. For a long time travelers came as far as Wellfleet by stagecoach and then by vessel the rest of the way. Not until later did the stagecoach lurch to Provincetown around the sand hills of the Eastern Harbor."

"Cape Cod Potato Chips was another beneficiary of the Demoulases' openness to local producers. Like Ken's, it offered a high-quality product but did not have deep enough pockets to break into other chains. Market Basket took Cape Cod early on, helping it grow into a nationally recognized brand."

Author: Daniel Korschun

"Second-guessing a Red Sox manager is like bemoaning Cape Cod traffic – it's a time-honored summer ritual."

Author: Anonymous

All About Sandwich

Sandwich is a town in Barnstable County, Massachusetts, and is the oldest town on Cape Cod. The town motto is Post tot Naufracia Portus, "after so many shipwrecks, a haven." The population was 20,259 at the 2020 census.

Cape Cod was inhabited for thousands of years by Native Americans prior to European colonization.

A group of English settlers from Saugus, Massachusetts, colonized Sandwich in 1637 with the permission of the Plymouth Colony. It is named for the seaport of Sandwich, Kent, England. It was incorporated in 1639 and is the oldest town on Cape Cod, together with Yarmouth. The western portion of the town was separated from the original Town of Sandwich and became the town of Bourne in 1884.

There are many historic homes in Sandwich, including the Benjamin Nye Homestead on Old County Road (formerly known as Old King's Highway) and the Benjamin Holway House built in 1789 at 379 Route 6A. This property hosts one of the original Nye Homestead structures built in 1698, believed to have originally served as either a tavern or a shop. It is now used as a law office.

Sandwich was the site of an early Quaker settlement and today hosts the oldest continuous Quaker Meeting in the U.S. There were some conflicts with other religious groups, and so some Quakers left the town for further settlements elsewhere, including Dartmouth, Massachusetts. Many of Sandwich's prominent families have Quaker ties.

Early industry revolved around agriculture, with fishing and trading also providing for the town. Later, the town grew a small industrial component along the Scusset River and Old Harbor Creek and its tributaries. Today, most of its industry revolves around tourism.

Deming Jarves founded the **Boston & Sandwich Glass Factory** in 1825. Sandwich had proximity to a shallow harbor, and had local supplies of timber to fuel the glass furnaces. The glass works primarily made lead glass and was known for its use of color. Jarves received several patents for his improvements in glass mold designs and pressing techniques. The factory declined after the American Civil War due to competition from Ohio, Pennsylvania, and West Virginia companies that produced less expensive pressed soda-lime glass tableware.

The **Cape Cod Canal** was constructed through the town starting in 1909, opening for travel in 1914. The Canal Generating Plant went online in 1968.

The town is also the location of the **Shawme-Crowell State Forest** and the Massachusetts State Game Farm. The town is home to six beaches along the shores of Cape Cod Bay. The rest of the town's geography is typical of the rest of the Cape, with many small ponds and hills, with most of the trees being pine or oak. Sandwich is also the site of Old Harbor Creek, a large inlet with several other small creeks feeding it, which once served to provide safe harbor for ships.

The Hoxie House in Sandwich provides a glimpse of the colonial past of Cape Cod. The house was constructed in a "saltbox-style" with two stories and a steep roof that mirrored an actual salt box.

People of Significance – Sandwich

Edmund Freeman (c. July 25, 1596–1682) was one of the founders of Sandwich, Massachusetts and an Assistant Governor of Plymouth Colony from 1640 to 1647, serving under Governor William Bradford and Governor Edward Winslow.

Freeman was the son of Edmund and Alice (Coles) Freeman of Pulborough, Sussex, England and was baptized July 25, 1596. Edmund married firstly to Bennett Hodsoll on June 16, 1617; she was buried at Pulborough on April 12, 1630. Freeman along with his second wife Elizabeth and his family set sail from Plymouth, England, on June 4, 1635, aboard the Abigail. During the crossing, an epidemic of smallpox broke out on shipboard. They arrived in Boston on October 8, 1635, and then settled in Saugus.

Edmund (or Edmond) Freeman was admitted freeman at Plymouth on January 23, 1637.

He was one of the ten founders of Sandwich. Freeman died in 1682 in Sandwich. He is buried in a well-known, marked private burial plot in Sandwich along with his second wife Elizabeth.

Thornton Waldo Burgess (January 17, 1874 – June 5, 1965) was an American conservationist and author of children's stories. Burgess loved the beauty of nature and its living creatures so much that he wrote about them for 50 years in books and his newspaper column, *Bedtime Stories*. He was sometimes known as the **Bedtime Story-Man**. By the time he retired, he had written more than 170 books and 15,000 stories for the daily newspaper column.

Born January 17, 1874, in Sandwich on Cape Cod, Burgess was the son of Caroline F. Haywood and Thornton W. Burgess Sr., a direct descendant of Thomas Burgess, one of the first Sandwich settlers in 1637. Thornton, Sr., died the same year his son was born, and the young Thornton, Jr. was brought up by his mother in Sandwich. They lived in humble circumstances. As a youth, he worked tending cows, picking trailing arbutus (mayflowers) or berries, shipping water lilies from local ponds, selling candy, and trapping muskrats. William C. Chipman, one of his employers, lived on Discovery Hill Road, a wildlife habitat of woodland and wetland. This habitat became the setting of many stories in which Burgess refers to Smiling Pool and the Old Briar Patch.

Graduating from **Sandwich High School** in 1891, Burgess briefly attended a business college in Boston from 1892 to 1893, living in Somerville, Massachusetts, at that time. But he disliked studying business and wanted to be an author. He relocated to Springfield, Massachusetts, where he accepted a job as an editorial assistant at the Phelps Publishing Company. His first stories were written using the pseudonym "W. B. Thornton."

Burgess married **Nina Osborne** in 1905, but she died in childbirth a year later, leaving him to raise their son alone. It is said that he began writing bedtime stories to entertain his young son, Thornton III. Burgess remarried in 1911; his wife Fannie had two children by a previous marriage. The couple later bought a home in Hampden, Massachusetts, in 1925 that became Burgess' permanent residence in 1957. His second wife died in August 1950. Burgess returned frequently to Sandwich, which he always claimed as his spiritual home. Many of his childhood experiences and the people he knew there influenced his interest and were the impetus for his concern for wildlife.

Nathaniel Freeman, Jr. (May 1, 1766 – August 22, 1800) was a United States Representative from Massachusetts. Born in Sandwich in the Province of Massachusetts Bay, he attended the common schools, graduated from Harvard University in 1787, and studied law. He was admitted to the bar about 1791 and commenced practice in Sandwich and the Cape Cod district. He served as brigade major in the Massachusetts militia for sixteen years, and was a justice of the peace in 1793.

Freeman was elected as a Federalist to the Fourth Congress and elected as a Democratic-Republican to the Fifth Congress, serving from March 4, 1795, to March 3, 1799. He died in Sandwich; interment was in the Old Burial Ground.

Do You Know – Sandwich?

Heritage Museums and Gardens (100 acres) is located at 67 Grove Street, Sandwich. The public garden, with its nationally significant collection of rhododendrons hybridized by Charles Dexter, over 1,000 varieties of daylilies and extensive hosta collection, is complemented by three gallery buildings containing a world-class collection of American automobiles, American folk art and a working 1919 carousel and rare carousel figures.

The **Wing Fort House**, located in East Sandwich, is recognized as the oldest home in New England continuously owned by the same family.

The house was built in 1641 and added to the National Register of Historic Places in 1976.

Hoxie House (ca. 1675) in Sandwich is one of the oldest houses on Cape Cod and one of the oldest surviving houses in Massachusetts.

The saltbox house was built in the mid-seventeenth century and occupied around 1675 by Rev. John Smith, his wife Susanna and their 13 children.

In the mid-nineteenth century, Abraham Hoxie, a whaling captain, purchased the property. The town of Sandwich acquired the home in the 1950s and restored the building.

Dexter Grist Mill, at the intersection of Main and Water streets in Sandwich, was built in 1654, fully restored in 1961, and got a new, larger **waterwheel** in 2015. It is the oldest grist mill on Cape Cod.

Thomas Dexter built the first grist mill on this site in 1654 so that the inhabitants of the village of Sandwich would not have to grind their own corn for cornmeal, their staple food.

Today you can buy cornmeal ground in the mill, along with recipes for dishes like those the early inhabitants of Sandwich might have made daily.

The **Daniel Webster Inn** has offered Cape Cod lodging for over three hundred years. Canopy and four-poster beds, fireplaces and oversized whirlpool tubs await your arrival. Each of the forty-eight guest rooms and suites is individually appointed with exquisite furnishings. Luxurious fireplace suites feature oversized whirlpool tubs, heated tile floors and the exclusive Suite Dreams Experience providing pampering amenities.

It was originally used as a parsonage for the Reverend Rowland Cotton and his wife, Elizabeth Saltonstall. Later it became home to the Reverend Fessenden who passed away at an early age leaving behind his wife and seven children. The home was then given to his family and a new home was purchased for Reverend Fessenden's successor.

The Fessenden family built an addition onto the home and operated the Cape Cod inn as the Fessenden Tavern from the mid 1700s until the 1800s. The Fessenden Tavern was known as the patriot headquarters during the Revolutionary period.

The most notable visitor was Daniel Webster, one of the most prominent men of his day. He had a room reserved at this Tavern from 1815 to 1851. Daniel Webster was a successful Boston lawyer who possessed a commanding personality and quick wit. He was an exceptional orator, winning most of the cases he defended. Daniel Webster also served several terms as a U.S. Senator

The **Belfry Inn & Bistro** features three historic buildings: The Abbey, The 1827 Village Inn, and The Painted Lady. While you cannot go wrong with spending the night in any of these buildings, all of which offer historic charm and exquisite amenities in Massachusetts, there is something extraordinary about The Painted Lady. The Painted Lady, a gorgeous Victorian home, once served as a church rectory. Built in 1882, the whimsical architecture features gables, a colorful exterior, and plenty of Victorian details that will transport you back in time.

The Abbey, a former church built in 1901, features six guest rooms and the Belfry's award-winning Bistro, while the 1827 Village is a converted boarding house with four rooms.

East Sandwich Meetinghouse. This is the home of the oldest continuous Quaker meeting in America, begun in 1656–1657. Schnell notes:

"Quakers migrated to Cape Cod from Boston to escape Puritan persecution."

The **Shawnee-Crowell State Forest** is a 700-acre pitch pine and scrub oak forest is located on the western end of Cape Cod and offers more than fifteen miles of trails for hiking and horseback riding. Camping is a favorite activity from early summer to the fall. Entrance can be found at 42 Main St., Sandwich.

Sandwich is also home to a major portion of **Otis Air National Guard Base**, including half the land that the runways are on.

The **Sandwich Boardwalk** is located in downtown and leads to the Town Beach on Cape Cod Bay. It is a popular tourist attraction and was elected by National Geographic in July 2010 as one of the top ten boardwalks in the United States. It is 1,350 feet long, from Scorton Creek to the Cape Cod Canal, and crossing the Creek Mill and the marsh. It was created in 1875. It was rebuilt in 1992, financed through the sale of 1,700 personalized planks with engravings. It was damaged by blizzards in March 2018 but was rebuilt and reopened in June 2018.

The glass making industry was first organized in 1825 and prospered for almost one hundred years. It relied on sand from canals in the area rather than beach sand. Its history in Sandwich is preserved at the **Sandwich Glass Museum**.

The Bulb River located on the grounds of the Heritage Museums & Gardens in Sandwich is a stunning view of 35,000 bright purple hyacinths that create a view that very much resembles a river. It even has eddies that are made of 1,500 yellow daffodils.

Titcomb's Book Shop in East Sandwich is one of those book stores memorable for the thoughtfulness and courtesy of the people who work there. They know their books and there is something for readers young and old. There are plenty of books and an excellent selection of games.

There is a **winter only campsite in Sandwich**. You can park a camper van at the campsite or you can pitch a tent right on the beach. There is no electricity, no indoor bathroom (though there is a portable toilet), or water hookups. What you are paying for is the ability to camp on the sand and build a fire without getting in trouble with the police. It is available through Airbnb.com.

Sandwich Fish Hatchery is located along Rte 6A because of the artesian springs supplying cold, clean water from the Cape Cod aquifer. Over 50,000 pounds of catchable rainbow, brook and brown trout are annually produced by this hatchery and stocked into ponds and rivers, primarily on Cape Cod and nearby areas.

The **Green Briar Nature Center & Jam Kitchen** pays homage to the works of children's' author Thornton Burgess, who grew up in the town of Sandwich. During his lifetime, Burgess penned more than a hundred books chronicling the tales of Peter Rabbit and his friends. The conservation area preserves the famous briar patch that appeared in many of Burgess's most beloved stories. Green Briar Conservation Area is a quiet corner of Cape Cod that encompasses nearly 60 acres of wildflower gardens, forests, and walking trails in East Sandwich. The Green Briar Nature Center and Jam Kitchen, which is located just next to the garden, carries on this mission by running natural history programs for all ages. These fascinating programs include guided walks of the gardens, field trips, and workshops on the natural sciences.

The Cape Cod Canal Visitor's Center is located in Sandwich. It contains the full history of the Canal including, videos, film, documents, and pictures about the Canal. There are interactive exhibitions and a 40 foot long patrol boat, the Renier. The reason for the Canal was that it saved 166 miles off the journey between Boston and New York for ships. Previous to the Canal being built, the ships had to go around Cape Cod through some treacherous waters.

All About Truro

Truro /ˈtrɜːroʊ/ is a town in Barnstable County comprising two villages: Truro and North Truro. Located slightly more than 100 miles by road from Boston, it is a summer vacation community just south of the northern tip of Cape Cod, in an area known as the "Outer Cape." English colonists named it after Truro in Cornwall, United Kingdom.

The historic **Wampanoag Native American** people called the area Pamet or Payomet. Their language was part of the large Algonquian family. This name was adopted for the Pamet River and the harbor area around the town center known as the Pamet Roads.

Truro was settled by English immigrant colonists in the 1690s as the northernmost portion of the town of Eastham. The town was officially separated and incorporated in 1709.

Fishing, whaling and shipbuilding made up the town's early industry. These industries had to shift to other locations as the harsh tides of the Lower Cape reduced the town's main port in the 1850s. In the late 19th and early 20th century, Cape Cod was a popular location for artists because of its light.

The population of Truro was 2,454 at the 2020 census.

Over half of the land area of the town is part of the **Cape Cod National Seashore**, established in 1961 by President John F. Kennedy, and administered by the U.S. National Park Service.

The **Highland House Museum** occupies one of Truro's best-known landmarks, the old Highland House, a hotel built on the Highlands in 1907. Located near the Highland Light in North Truro, it is a classic example of a turn-of-the-century summer resort hotel. The Highland House is owned by the Truro Historical Society. The Museum has collections pertaining to shipwrecks that occurred of the coast of Truro.

Fishing, whaling and shipbuilding made up the town's early industry. These industries had to shift to other locations as the harsh tides of the Lower Cape reduced the town's main port in the 1850s. In the late 19th and early 20th century, Cape Cod was a popular location for artists because of its light.

Gentlemen from Truro were sent to Nantucket to **teach the islanders** the art of killing whales and blackfish. In the 1800s, small shipbuilding in the harbor, fishing, salt-works through the use of windmills, combined with large gardens made for a good life in this small hamlet.

Shortly after World War II, the Federal Government straightened and rebuilt **Route 6**. Millions and millions of people were now a days drive away. On many days during the summer season Truro may have as many as 15,000 people enjoying the sun, the woods, and the beach.

Because of the creation of the **National Seashore** in 1960 two-thirds of Truro is preserved in its natural state.

> "Diane is my spiritual guide. She is a Duke- and Harvard-educated oyster fisherman in Cape Cod. Now there's something you don't hear every day. Like Jackie and Doug, she does not seek the spotlight."
>
> Author: Megyn Kelly

People of Significance – Truro

The English Pilgrims stopped in Truro and Provincetown in 1620 as their original choice for a landing before later deciding the area to be unsuitable. They were led by **Miles Standish**. While there, they discovered fresh water and corn stored by the Wampanoag. Historians debate the accuracy of the account about the latter discovery, but in popular lore it led to the place being called Corn Hill.

Truro was settled by **English immigrant colonists** in the 1690s as the northernmost portion of the town of Eastham. The town was officially separated and incorporated in 1709.

Artist Edward Hopper owned a summer house in Truro, and painted numerous Truro scenes including *Corn Hill* (1930), *Highland Light, North Truro* (1930), and *Cottages at North Truro* (1936).

Edward Knight Collins was born on August 5, 1802, in Truro. The Collins Line is the common name for the American shipping company started by Israel Collins and then built up by his son Edward Knight Collins, formally called the New York and Liverpool United States Mail Steamship Company.

Do You Know – Truro?

The **English Pilgrims** stopped in Truro and Provincetown in 1620 as their original choice for a landing before later deciding the area to be unsuitable. While there, they discovered fresh water and corn stored by the Wampanoag. Historians debate the accuracy of the account about the latter discovery, but in popular lore it led to the name Corn Hill.

Truro is one of the more exclusive towns on the Cape, noted for its affluent residences and the rolling hills and dunes along the coast. It is the site of the **Highland Light** (also known as the Cape Cod Light), the earliest lighthouse on Cape Cod. The first building was erected in 1797; the current lighthouse was built in 1857. The entire 430-ton light was moved by 1/10 of a mile inland in 1996. By then, because of erosion, its original site was just ten yards from the edge of the shore cliffs.

Off Head of the Meadow beach on the Atlantic side of Truro lies the ship wreck of the three masted barque Frances. The Hamburg-based **ship wrecked** off Truro on December 27, 1872, while on her way from the Far East to Boston. Usually submerged, the wreck will appear when weather and tides line up.

North Truro is home to **Truro Vineyards**, one of two operating wineries (the other is in Falmouth) on Cape Cod. Located on Shore Road, Truro Vineyards opens their doors to wine lovers from around the world to enjoy wine tastings and free guided tours of the vineyard and winery, including a state of the art barrel room. Learn about the art of maritime grape growing, and its yield of intense flavor and lush varietal character. Check their online calendar for fun events.

North Truro is also home to **Highlands Links Golf Course**, Massachusetts's oldest links course. The course runs along the highland cliffs on the Atlantic coast and encompasses the Highland Light.

Nike-Hydac launch site is located at North Truro Air Force Station on Cape Cod, and was in use between 1969-1970. Starting in 1969 the

Missile and Drone Division of the Air Force Missile Development Center (Holloman AFB) was tasked to support the development of sensors at MIT. It was determined that it would be more cost effective to have a launch site in the New England area rather than attempt to move the sensor to Holloman AFB/White Sands Missile Range. A site was located at North Truro Air Force Station. Under the code name Have Horn, a sounding rocket launcher and associated equipment was installed at that station. The first Nike-Hydac sounding rocket was launched from that site in December 1969 and followed with a few more in the early 1970s. All launches were successful. Following the launches, all equipment was air-lifted back to Holloman AFB. Wayne O. Mattson was launch control officer for this exercise.

Paradise Hollow is a trip back in time, somehow sealed in by the creation of the Cape Cod National Seashore. There are no houses, just trees, hills, and room to daydream about bears and pirates. Just what the doctor ordered!

There is an abandoned **1950s neighborhood** and military installation in North Truro, just as it was in the 1950s. It is the North Truro Air Force Station located off Route 6 at the Highland Light Exit in North Truro.

An 865-pound Revere Foundry bell, suspended in the steeple of the **1827 Meeting House**, is one of the last bells cast by the famous foundry established by the famed patriot, Paul Revere.

Truro is home to **Chequessett Chocolate**, a well-known chocolatier at 8 Highland Road in North Truro. A trained chef and Cape Cod native from a long line of captains and fisherman opened the chocolate factory in 2014, and has become a meeting place for locals and tourists alike.

Atlantic Spice Company, located at 2 Shore Road in North Truro, is one of the best suppliers on the East Coast for herbs and spices and is worth a visit. The retail store has become a destination for summer visitors to the Outer Cape, as well as an opportunity for year-round customers to engage in some retail therapy during the long, cold Cape Cod winter.

Payomet Performing Arts Center produces exciting professional live music, theatre, circus arts and humanities events rooted in strong social values. Located at Highlands Center at Cape Cod National Seashore, Payomet is something to experience.

> "Cape Cod is the bared and bended arm of Massachusetts. The shoulder is at Buzzard's Bay; the elbow at Cape Mallebarre; the wrist at Truro; and the sandy fist at Provincetown."
>
> Author: Henry David Thoreau

All About Wellfleet

Wellfleet is a town in Barnstable County located halfway between the "tip" and "elbow" of Cape Cod. The town had a population of 3,566 at the 2020 census, which swells nearly sixfold during the summer. A total of 70 percent of the town's land area is under protection, and nearly half of it is part of the Cape Cod National Seashore. Wellfleet is famous for its oysters, which are celebrated in the annual October Wellfleet OysterFest.

The area was originally settled by Europeans in the 1650s as Billingsgate (after the famous fish market in East London). In 1717, the pirate "Black Sam" Bellamy was sailing nearby when his ship, the Whydah, sank offshore, together with over 4.5 short tons of gold and silver and all but two of its 145 men. The wreck was discovered in 1984, the first of only two confirmed pirate shipwrecks ever to have been discovered.

Wellfleet was part of neighboring Eastham until 1763 when it achieved town status after nearly 30 years of petitioning. Wellfleet's oyster beds drove the early economy, as did whaling and fishing. The town was home to 30 whaling ships at the time of the American Revolution.

Because of the decline of whaling and the mackerel catch in the late 19th century, the fleet declined, being completely free of schooners by 1900. The oyster fleet continued, however, and many types of shellfish continue to be harvested. Despite this decline, a church near the town center continues to operate a clock that chimes ship's time.

People of Significance – Wellfleet

Lorenzo Dow Baker (March 15, 1840 in Wellfleet, Massachusetts – June 21, 1908) was an American sailor, ship's captain and businessman whose 1870 voyage from the Orinoco to Jamaica and then to Philadelphia launched the modern banana production industry. In 1881 he partnered with his brother-in-law Elisha Hopkins to form L.D. Baker & Co. In 1885 he joined forces with Andrew W. Preston and eight others to form the Boston Fruit Company, which led to several successive partnerships, ending in the 1899 formation of the United Fruit Company, now Chiquita Brands International. Baker's success caused Wellfleet to become a summer resort. Baker left a fortune of $4 million (equivalent to $115,214,815 in 2020) upon his death in 1908.

Captain Samuel Bellamy (c. February 23, 1689 – April 26, 1717), later known as **"Black Sam" Bellamy**, was an English Sailor, turned pirate, who operated in the early 18th century. He is best known as the wealthiest pirate in recorded history. In 1717, Bellamy took a captured vessel as his own, before capturing a state-of-the-art slave trade ship, the Whydah Gally, in the early spring of 1717. Two months later, the vessel was caught in a nor'easter storm off the coast of Massachusetts and sank, taking Bellamy and most of his crew down with it. The remains of the Whydah Gally were discovered in 1984, making it the first authenticated pirate ship discovered in North America.

In 1793, **Levi Whitman**, Wellfleet's minister, wrote "A Topographical Description of Wellfleet" that is preserved today in the records of the Massachusetts Historical Society. He wrote about Wellfleet, "The inhabitants do not raise grain sufficient for the town. The common method is to import it from the southern states. We have for grinding it into meal, five windmills and one tide mill."

Constance Hopkins and Nicholas Snow started this Mayflower family. Constance was the **Mayflower traveler**, arriving in Plymouth when she was a teenager. One of her descendants, Sylvanus Snow, settled in South Wellfleet, along with a brother named Samuel.

Do You Know – Wellfleet?

In front of the Wellfleet Beachcomber is one of those hidden spots that locals love to rave about, **a beautiful beach that is not crowded**. It is blessed with limited parking and a remote location.

Guglielmo Marconi built America's **first transatlantic radio transmitter station** on a coastal bluff in South Wellfleet in 1901–02. The first radio telegraph transmission from America to England was sent from this station on January 18, 1903, a ceremonial telegram from President Theodore Roosevelt to King Edward VII. Three quarters of the land it originally encompassed has been eroded into the sea. The South Wellfleet station's first call sign was "CC" for Cape Cod. The Marconi receiving station was in Marion, Massachusetts.

Wellfleet has the second greatest concentration of **art galleries** on Cape Cod, right after Provincetown.

The Cape Cod National Seashore circles the town, from Jeremy Point through the marshes and "islands" along the Herring River, includes Cahoon Hollow Beach, and extends the length of the Atlantic shore of the town.

The **Atlantic White Cedar Swamp** in Wellfleet will make you feel like you have stepped into a fantasy realm worthy of J.R.R. Tolkien. It begins in a stunted oak and pine forest filled with lively sounds of wildlife and takes you through mature woodland to one of the most breathtaking areas in Massachusetts, the Atlantic White Cedar Swamp. It was created during the last Ice Age and features a layer of peat 24 feet deep. The massive, towering trees have remarkably straight trunks.

In 1717, the pirate vessel Whydah sank off the coast of Wellfleet with plunder from 50 ships on board. Explorer Barry Clifford discovered the wreck site in 1984 and has since pulled up 200,000 artifacts, including gold ornaments, sword handles, even a boy's leg. It is the only **authenticated pirate shipwreck** in America.

Recently discovered Colonial-era documents suggest the Whydah raided two vessels before it sank and that 400,000 gold coins are still unaccounted for.

If you have ever wanted to step onto a real pirate ship, a visit to the **Whydah Pirate Museum** is your chance. This museum is centered around the infamous Whydah, a pirate vessel that sank off the coast of Wellfleet in 1717. Visitors can explore a full-scale replica of the ship and immerse themselves in the world of pirates.

Great Island is connected to the mainland by a narrow strip of land known as "The Gut," with the Wellfleet Harbor on one side and the Cape Cod Bay on the other. It is home to a little-known beach and is worth getting to with a bit of hiking. The parking lot is where Chequesset Neck Road and Griffin Island Road meet. Plan on 3-5 hours to explore.

Great Island Trail follows sandy stretches between the elevated heights of Great Island and Great Beach Hill. Its higher elevations punctuate spectacular vistas which emerge from an even-aged, pitch-pine forest. Part of this trail leads to a colonial-era tavern site (no remains visible). Other sections skirt salt marsh embayments.

The Wellfleet Drive-In is one of the venues for the annual Provincetown International Film Festival in Provincetown. Frommer's lists the Drive-In as one of the "500 Places to See Before They Disappear." The Drive-In also hosts the popular **Wellfleet Flea Market**, with up to 150 vendors during the summer months.

Wellfleet is so renowned for its oysters that thousands of people visit each year for the **Wellfleet OysterFest**. For two days each fall, the town celebrates clam, oyster, and shellfishing traditions.

Herridge Books features books for every member of the family. The titles are priced individually and arranged by section. Do not be surprised if you walk out with more than you planned to buy.

The **bells at the First Congregational Church** on Main Street ring every half hour. This occurs because the church is home to the only bell clock in the U.S. that remains on ship's time. On a ship, time is broken into four-hour shifts that start in the AM and PM at 12:00, 4:00, and 8:00. There is one bell-ring for every half hour past the start of a shift.

All About Yarmouth

Yarmouth (/ˈjɑːrməθ/ YAR-məth) is a town in Barnstable County, Massachusetts, United States, Barnstable County being coextensive with Cape Cod. The population was 23,793 at the 2010 census.

The town is made up of three major villages: South Yarmouth, West Yarmouth, and Yarmouth Port. Wampanoag origins.

Prior to European settlement, Yarmouth was inhabited by the Wampanoag, an Algonquian people. In the Wôpanâak language the area was called "Mattacheese." Wampanoag tribes living in Yarmouth at the time of European settlement included the Pawkunnawkuts on both sides of the lower Bass River, the Hokanums in what is now northeastern Yarmouth, and the Cummaquids in what is now western Yarmouth.

Yarmouth was organized and incorporated as part of the Plymouth Colony on September 3, 1639, following a settlement led by John Crowe (later Crowell), Thomas Howes and Anthony Thacher, and is, together with Sandwich, the oldest town on Cape Cod. Yarmouth originally included what is now the town of Dennis, which was incorporated as a separate community on June 19, 1793.

Yarmouth is named after Great Yarmouth, a town in the county of Norfolk, on the east coast of England, which is itself at the mouth of the River Yare.

In 1642 and 1645, Yarmouth furnished soldiers for the Plymouth Colony's expeditions against the Narragansett. In 1648, the Plymouth Colony's legislature, the General Court, appointed Myles Standish to adjudicate land disputes among the Yarmouth settlers. Yarmouth soldiers served the Plymouth Colony in King Philip's War: fifteen Yarmouth men participated in the Great Swamp Fight without casualties, but the town did lose five men at Rehoboth. Yarmouth troops also saw service in the early years of King William's War. In the early eighteenth century, some of the Yarmouth veterans of King Philip's War were granted lands to settle in Gorham, Maine.

Yarmouth was the site of an active group of the Sons of Liberty during the American Revolution. The town's militia mustered to provide assistance to the minutemen at the Battles of Lexington and Concord, but the militia returned home upon news that the rebels had already triumphed on the field. In March 1776, Yarmouth troops served as part of George Washington's forces during the Fortification of Dorchester Heights. A meeting of Yarmouth citizens declared the town's independence from Great Britain on June 20, 1776. As a coastal community, Yarmouth was subject to blockade by the Royal Navy throughout the Revolutionary War.

In the early years of the Republic, Yarmouth shared with the rest of New England a strong support for the Federalist Party. The economy of Yarmouth was centered on maritime industries, and the townspeople were consequently opposed to the Jefferson Administration's Embargo Act of 1807 and Non-Intercourse Act of 1809.

On July 8, 1812, the Yarmouth town meeting voted to protest the recent Congressional declaration of war with Great Britain. Along with much of the rest of coastal New England, Yarmouth was subject to blockade by the Royal Navy beginning in 1814.

Yarmouth began as a farming community in which the people of the town raised pigs, cattle, and sheep. Due to livestock pasturage, firewood collection, shipbuilding, and the construction of the Old Colony Railroad, the old-growth forests of the Wampanoag era had disappeared from Yarmouth.

Although agriculture was a prominent part of Yarmouth life, the town's location led its people to make much of their living from the ocean.

Developers began to refashion Yarmouth into a summer resort near the end of the nineteenth century. Hotels and summer cottage communities proliferated in the first half of the twentieth century, particularly along what is now Route 28 With the emergence of the car culture in the years just after World War II, these were joined first by many motels (mostly along Route 28 in West Yarmouth) and later by the denser, suburban pattern of residential housing construction that characterizes Yarmouth today.

People of Significance – Yarmouth

Asa Eldridge (1809–1856) was a sea captain from Yarmouth. In 1854, Captain Eldridge guided the clipper ship Red Jacket from New York and to Liverpool in only in 13 days, 1 hour, and 25 minutes, dock to dock, setting a speed record for the fastest trans-Atlantic crossing by a commercial sailing vessel that has remained unbroken ever since. In 1856, Captain Eldridge skippered the ill-fated steamship SS Pacific, which disappeared at sea on a voyage from Liverpool to New York.

Eldridge is also known for having captained Cornelius Vanderbilt's private steam-powered yacht, the North Star, when the tycoon took a small group of family and friends on a summer-long cruise around Europe in 1853.

Lot Hall (April 2, 1757 – May 17, 1809) was a Vermont attorney, politician, and judge. A veteran of the American Revolution, Hall served as a Justice of the Vermont Supreme Court from 1794 to 1800. His name sometimes appears in written records as "Lott Hall."

Lot Hall was born in Yarmouth on April 2, 1757. He received his early education in Barnstable County, Massachusetts, though the exact circumstances are unknown. He identified with the Patriot cause at the start of the American Revolution, and in May 1776 he enlisted in the United States Navy. Hall was a member of a force raised in New England by Captain Robert Cochran and Lieutenant Elijah Freeman Payne for the defense of the South Carolina coast; promised a lieutenant's commission if he recruited 15 others, Hall enlisted 30.

Upon returning to Massachusetts, Hall began to study law with Shearjashub Bourne; he was admitted to the bar in 1782, and relocated to Westminster, Vermont. In addition to practicing law, he quickly became involved in the government of the Vermont Republic.

Joseph Eldridge Hamblin (January 13, 1828 – July 3, 1870) was an American officer during the Civil War, who led a regiment and then a brigade in the Army of the Potomac.

Hamblin, the son of Benjamin and Hannah (Sears) Hamblin, was born January 13, 1828 at Yarmouth. He was an insurance broker at the outbreak of the war. Long a member of the 7th New York Volunteer Infantry Regiment, then the 7th Regiment of the New York militia, he enlisted in 1861.

When **Colonel Alexander Shaler** became a general, Hamblin became regimental colonel in his place. He especially distinguished himself at the Battle of Cedar Creek, where he was wounded while leading a brigade of VI Corps. Hamblin was brevetted as a brigadier general and in 1865 promoted to full rank, with the brevet of major general for gallantry at Battle of Sailor's Creek.

After the war he was prominent in the New York National Guard and resumed work in the insurance business.

George Thatcher (April 12, 1754 – April 6, 1824) was an American lawyer, jurist, and statesman from the Maine district of Massachusetts. His name sometimes appears as **George Thacher**. He was a delegate for Massachusetts to the Continental Congress in 1787 and 1788. He was an associate justice of the Massachusetts Supreme Judicial Court from 1801 to 1824.

Thatcher was born April 12, 1754, in Yarmouth in the Province of Massachusetts Bay. After private tutoring, he attended Harvard, graduating in 1776. He read law and was admitted to the bar in 1778, and then moved to York in Massachusetts' District of Maine to open a practice. By 1782 he had settled in Biddeford.

Thatcher was named as one of the Massachusetts delegates to the Continental Congress in 1787. He wrote under the name "Scribble Scrabble."

Capt. Ebenezer Sears, of Yarmouth in 1854, was the first American to take a merchant vessel around the Cape of Good Hope.

In 1854, **Captain Asa Eldridge** of Yarmouth skippered the clipper Red Jacket, a packet ship, between New York and Liverpool in only 13 days, 1 hour, and 25 minutes, dock to dock, setting a speed record.

Do You Know – Yarmouth?

Approaching Yarmouth, you will enter **The Captains' Mile**. Curving and meandering, the road runs past historic inns and old stone walls covered with lichen ... while stretching out along both sides sit over fifty homes once owned by Sea Captains. You can easily identify them because they all bear the distinctive oval, black and gold Schooner Plaque awarded by the Historical Society of Old Yarmouth.

This **Schooner Plaque** identifies a home once owned by a Sea Captain. Keep in mind that homes bearing the plaque are privately owned and not open to the public. However the only furnished Sea Captain's home on Cape Cod regularly open to the public is *The Captain Bangs Hallet House Museum*, less than a hundred yards off The Captains' Mile at 11 Strawberry Lane in Yarmouth Port.

The headquarters of the **International Fund for Animal Welfare (IFAW),** a global animal welfare and conservation charity founded in 1969, is located in Yarmouth Port. The organization works to rescue individual animals, safeguard populations, preserve habitat, and advocate for greater protections. Brian Davies founded IFAW. IFAW was instrumental in ending the commercial seal hunt in Canada. In 1983 Europe banned all whitecoat harp seals products. This ban helped save over one million seals. IFAW operates in over forty countries.

Parnassus Book Store in Yarmouthport is a general book store selling new and old (often rare) books as well as issuing specialty catalogs on a variety of subjects: Americana, Latin America, Maritime, Art, the Orient and a variety of other subjects. The store is known for its outdoor book stall (leave your money under the door) and shelves that hold books you never expected to find.

In 1970, the national **Christmas Tree Shops** retail chain was founded at a location on Route 6A in Yarmouth Port. It is an American chain of specialty retail stores headquartered in Union, New Jersey. As of 2021, the chain operates eighty stores in twenty U.S. states.

The **Taylor–Bray Farm** is a farm in Yarmouth Port and was originally owned and settled by Richard "of the Rock" Taylor in 1639 while it was still part of Plymouth colony. Stephen Hopkins, a distant maternal line ancestor, was given permission to build a house and cut hay near this farm in 1638, but the first house in Yarmouth built by an Englishman was built by his son Giles in 1638.

The last owner to work the farm was Robert J Williams who in 1946 purchased the farm and eighty-eight acres for the tax due on the property. The Town of Yarmouth to purchase the property in 1987 with the intention "to maintain the farm for historic preservation and conservation." Tenant/managers now live in the farmhouse, welcoming the public and educating school groups about the farm's history and natural environment.

The **Yarmouth Sand Sculpture Trail** meanders through all of the villages of Yarmouth. The massive sculptures, which in total required more than 115 tons of sand, are on display in front of local businesses and landmarks. Most sculptures required about three tons of sand and a full day to complete. The sculptures are left up until October and are organized by the Yarmouth Chamber of Commerce.

Bass Hole Boardwalk is located at Gray's Beach in Yarmouth Port and is a supremely stunning spot. It was first built in the early 1900s and has been rebuilt several times after damage by storms. If you follow a dirt road called Alms House Rd. (being respectful of nearby private residences) there is a beautiful, secluded point overlooking Bass Creek and the marshes.

Bass Hole was the original hub of Yarmouth's maritime activities. But as the Hole started to silt in, maritime activities shifted west to the Mill Creek Area in West Yarmouth.

The most famous tree on Cape Cod is behind the Hallet House in Yarmouth Port. This is what visitors see: a giant room, 70 feet across, created by a tree – a European weeping beech. Branches dip and curve to create a green and grey sanctuary, a giant room with a cathedral ceiling. The canopy, perhaps 60 feet above, lets in just the right amount of light and warmth and the dense foliage allows playful breezes into the space. The thick, "weeping" branches twist throughout the room, some digging deep into the soil, others soaring just above head height. The scene evokes awe, making it little wonder that this quiet piece of history has often been chosen as the setting for wedding ceremonies.

Bass River is an estuary and village in South Yarmouth. The estuary separates the towns of Yarmouth and Dennis at the central, southern sections of the towns. At its widest and most southerly point, it opens to and meets Nantucket Sound. Its brackish, northwestern end flows into Follins Pond, winding further north as a brook to Mill Pond then as an underground stream that nearly bisects Cape Cod. The river was once considered a site for a cross cape Canal because it nearly bisects the Cape.

The **Whydah Pirate Museum** on Route 28 contains the only authenticated treasure on exhibit in the world.

The **Judah Baker Windmill** is an 18th-century windmill named after its original builder, Judah Baker, who built the mill in 1791. The windmill moved several times and is now located at 89 River Street in Bass River, located within the Historic District of South Yarmouth.

There is an old fashion soda fountain still operating in Yarmouth. It started life as an apothecary and drugstore, eventually expanding to offer classic home-cooked meals and even adding a soda fountain. Though it no longer serves as a pharmacy, **Hallet's** has been dishing up treats and soda since 1889. It is located at 139 Route 6A, Yarmouth Port.

Across a small bridge, nestled in its own secluded meadow sits what might first seem an apparition. Charming and unpretentious, clad in the shingles that mark so many structures on this peninsula is **Kelley Chapel**. Far from crowds and surrounded by nature trails – yet just steps from the Old King's Highway – it's a beautiful setting for your wedding ceremony. The Chapel seats 60 people and guests to a wedding held in the Chapel are greeted with a sign that reads, "Pick a Seat not a Side."

The Bud Carter Conservation area contains the highest point in Yarmouth: 118 feet above sea level. According to the Yarmouth Conservation Department, "'The trail is situated on the Sandwich Moraine, a significant glacially formed accumulation of unconsolidated glacial debris left over from the last ice age 20,000 years ago. Many large granite rocks dot the landscape, and a history of granite mining is evident by the drill holes made for blasting."

The house of another Yarmouth sea captain, **Captain Bangs Hallet**, is now a museum and home to the Historical Society of Old Yarmouth.

The Gorey House – a gorgeous old place on 6A in Yarmouth Port that was once the home of the brilliant author and illustrator Edward Gorey (1925-2000) is a museum dedicated to his life and work. Gorey is famous for his macabre tales and illustrations featuring doomed ballerinas, ill-fated children, sad-eyed monsters, and mustachioed dandies decked out in fur coats and old timey racing goggles. Gorey's humor is as dark as the blackest of nights, his language is delightful, eccentric, and addictive, and his drawings are crosshatched perfection.

Delve into Yarmouth history by way of the **Olde Cape Cod Discovery Trail**, which allows guests to walk or drive by its waterways through a self-guided tour. Stops include the Taylor Bray Farm (108 Bray Farm Road North, Yarmouth Port), a farmhouse constructed by early settlers, with artifacts from Native Americans that are thousands of years old; Ancient Cemetery (Center Street), which not only hosts a number of early settlers' graves, but also has the rock that designates the location of the First Congregational Church of Yarmouth.

The Cape Cod Rail Trail runs 25 miles from South Yarmouth to South Wellfleet. Offering plenty of space and largely shaded by trees, the Rail Trail can be enjoyed by the entire family. (Bike rental shops can be found in Yarmouth and along the trail.)

Best place to view the **sunset** in Yarmouth is from the boardwalk at Gray's (Bass Hole) Beach, at Center Street, Yarmouth.

The Callery Darling Conservation Area is located to the north of Route 6A in Yarmouth Port. Parking is available at several locations. The Callery Darling Conservation Area delights visitors with its beautiful views and ecological diversity. Abandoned cranberry bogs now support large red maple swamps. Ancient salt water bogs are also present with the original dikes still intact, and mature pine and oak forests disguise large areas of historic sand mining for the bogs.

Treasures of Cape Cod

I define "Treasures" as the places, institutions, organizations that make Cape Cod an incredibly special place for millions of people. Some are well known, and others are best known only by full and part time residents. I have selected the ones that, to me, and hopefully to the reader, qualify as special. After you have experienced them, you feel a sense of admiration and wonder. People who live on or visit Cape Cod are indeed fortunate to experience these incredibly special organizations, places and institutions.

Beaches

The main beaches on Cape Cod are well known, but in the 600 miles of oceanfront on Cape Cod are some lesser known, even secret beaches that add to the charm of Cape Cod and are well worth a visit.

Here is a list of the best big beaches as selected by *US News*. US News considered factors such as scenic beauty, facilities, nearby sights and expert and traveler opinions to determine the best Cape Cod beaches.

1. **Mayflower Beach** has beautiful views that make it a favorite among visitors of Dennis. At low tide, a visitor can walk for miles before reaching the sea.
2. **Marconi Beach** is in the Wellfleet section of the Cape Cod National Seashore. It has large sand dunes and is home to seals.
3. **Race Point Beach** is ideal for surfing, swimming, and sunbathing. You can find a Life Saving Station from the 1800s.
4. **Veterans Park Beach** in Hyannis is a wonderful place to watch boats passing by. A small beach but easily accessible.
5. **Old Silver Beach** in Falmouth offers calm, warm water with excellent views of the towns on the South Coast.
6. **Ballston Beach** is a family friendly beach in Truro that has consistent waves. It is usually not crowded.

7. **Sandy Neck Beach** spans six miles in Barnstable, one of the few that has an area designated for off road vehicles.
8. **Craigsville Beach** has a convenient location and offers showers, umbrellas, and handicap accessibility.
9. **Skaket Beach** is located on the Bay side of the Cape in Orleans. It offers warm water and a flat shore.
10. **Nauset Beach** is over ten miles in length in Orleans. It has sections for boogie boarding and surfing.
11. **Coast Guard Beach** located in Eastham has big waves for surfing and clam water for boogie boarding.
12. **Chatham Lighthouse Beach** is a large beach with splendid views but very limited parking and no lifeguards.
13. **West Dennis Beach** is long, flat with easy access and a large parking lot. There are many amenities available.

Small (Some Secret) Out of the Way Beaches

Cahoon Hollow Beach is a beach in Wellfleet, on the Cape Cod National Seashore. It lies in front of the Beachcomber restaurant and has limited parking so it is not crowed. It is surrounded by 75 ft. sand dunes.

Kalmus Beach in Hyannis is known for its white sand and clear waters with a range of visitor-friendly facilities, including restrooms and showers. Lifeguards are on duty during the summer up until Labor Day. It is surrounded by water on three sides and is known as a wind-surfer haven.

Bound Brook Island Beach is a very secluded beach in Wellfleet. It lies down about a mile at the end of Bound Brook Island Road in Wellfleet. At that point you can see the grass topped dunes and the always empty beach is just on the other side. It is also noted for its spectacular views.

Crowe's Pasture Beach is a secluded beach in Dennis, accessible by a mile long walk through the Crowe's Pasture Conservation Area. On the trail to the beach, you will pass marshlands and woods. The beach, a mix of sand, marshy lands and sea grass, is one of the more secluded spots on the entire Cape.

Princess Beach in Dennis is one of the few pond beaches in Dennis. It is a small, but very pleasant beach. There is a roped off area for swimming as well as a small playground making it an ideal spot for families with small children. It is accessible via the Princess Beach trail on Scargo Lake.

The Knob in Falmouth remains a hidden beach primarily because it is only accessible by a mile-long pedestrian causeway jutting out between Quissett Harbor and Buzzards Bay that leads to a little knob of land that is part of the area's 12-acre nature preserve.

Stony Beach, a hidden gem tucked away from the heart of Woods Hole Village. Despite its name the shore is mostly sandy. Make your way from the village center through the neighboring community, home to the Marine Biological Laboratory. Visit at low tide when you can wade out and try snorkeling in these shallow waters.

Monks Park, Pocasset, is part of the Little Bay Conservation area. Monk's Park on the Upper Cape offers a quiet corner to watch the tide flow in and out or take in some of the best sunsets on the entire Cape. It is more a hiking area than swimming hole. Visitors, if they see anyone at all, will encounter dog walkers, nature lovers and bird spotters.

Thumpertown Beach in Eastham can be found at the bottom of a wooden staircase. This small, secluded patch of sandy beach on the Outer Cape is known to amass sun worshippers during hot, summer months, but offseason it is a paradise for those taking a quiet run or walk down the coast with nothing but the sound of the sea and gulls in the distance. When the tide is out, enjoy the rolling sand bars and small tidal pools.

Spruce Hill Beach in Brewster has a one-half-mile trail leading to the ocean. The main trail is wide and straight and half way down you can veer off onto a single-track trail for a more scenic walk. Eventually, you are brought to a board walk and stairs over the dune to Cape Cod Bay. A Brewster Beach sticker is required to park, otherwise there is a $40 fine.

Cow Yard Landing in North Chatham is easy to find, as Cow Yard Landing sits in a residential area just off Old Harbor Road and close to Route 28. There is plenty of parking along Cow Yard Lane so you will not have to worry about searching for a spot. It is not crowded.

Cape Cod Museum of Natural History in Brewster is well worth the stroll. The seaside area is massive, with tons of white sand and space to stretch out away from the crowds. While you cannot park right at the museum, unless you are a paying customer, spots are available at Drummer Boy Park. From the park, it is a five-minute walk along Main Street, or Route 6, to the museum and then a short stroll along a marked trail to the water.

Cape Cod Baseball League

The **Cape Cod Baseball League** (**CCBL** or **Cape League**) is a collegiate summer baseball league. One of the nation's premier collegiate summer leagues, the league boasts over one thousand former players who have gone on to play in the major leagues. Cape Cod Baseball League alumni include Hall of Famers like Thurman Munson, Frank Thomas and Craig Biggio, Jacoby Ellsbury, Tim Lincecum and Mark Teixeira.

In 1963, the Cape Cod Baseball League was reorganized and became officially sanctioned by the NCAA. The league would no longer be limited to Cape Cod residents but would recruit college players and coaches from an increasingly wide radius.

In 1985, the league moved away from the use of aluminum bats, and became the only collegiate summer league in the nation at that time to use wooden bats. This transition began a period of significant growth in the league's popularity and prestige among MLB scouts, as well as among college players and coaches. This popularity has translated into over one thousand former players who have gone on to major league playing careers, including multiple members of the National Baseball Hall of Fame.

The CCBL regular season runs from mid-June through mid-August. Teams are geographically divided into the **East Division and West Division**. Each division consists of five teams which each play 44 regular season games, 6 games against each team from within their division, and 4 games against each team from the other division.

The West Division includes the Bourne Braves, Cotuit Kettleers, Falmouth Commodores, Hyannis Harbor Hawks, and Wareham Gatemen.

The East Division includes the Brewster Whitecaps, Chatham Anglers, Harwich Mariners, Yarmouth-Dennis Red Sox, and Orleans Firebirds.

Cape Cod Canal

The Cape Cod Canal is an artificial waterway connecting Cape Cod Bay in the north to Buzzards Bay in the south, and is part of the Atlantic Intracoastal Waterway. The approximately seven-mile-long canal traverses the neck of land joining Cape Cod to the state's mainland. It mostly follows tidal rivers widened to 480 feet and deepened to 32 feet at mean low water, shaving 135 miles off the journey around the Cape for its approximately 14,000 annual users. The canal is occasionally used by whales and dolphins including endangered North Atlantic right whales; these can cause closure of the canal.

Bridges over the Canal

The **Cape Cod Canal Railroad Bridge** (also known as the **Buzzards Bay Railroad Bridge**), a vertical lift bridge in Bourne near Buzzards Bay, carries railroad traffic across the Cape Cod Canal, connecting Cape Cod with the mainland.

The bridge was constructed beginning in 1933 by the Public Works Administration from a design by firms Parsons, Klapp, Brinckerhoff, and Douglas as well as Mead and White (both of New York), for the United States Army Corps of Engineers, which operates both the bridge and the canal.

The bridge has a 544-foot main span, with a 135-foot clearance when raised, uses 1,100-short-ton counterweights on each end, and opened on December 29, 1935. The bridge replaced a bascule bridge that had been built in 1910.

The Sagamore and Bourne Bridges

The **Sagamore Bridge** and its sibling the **Bourne Bridge** were constructed beginning in 1933 by the Public Works Administration for the U.S. Army Corps of Engineers, which operates both the bridges and the canal. Both bridges carry four lanes of traffic over a 616 feet main span, with a 135 feet ship clearance. They opened to traffic on June 22, 1935. The design of the Sagamore and Bourne bridges was later copied in miniature for the John Greenleaf Whittier Bridge that connects I-95 from Newburyport to Amesbury, Massachusetts.

The bridges replaced a drawbridge which was built before the canal was widened. The original bridge approaches are still visible to the north of the modern bridge, though both approaches are in low-traffic residential areas.

Cape Cod National Seashore

The **Cape Cod National Seashore**, created on August 7, 1961 by President John F. Kennedy, encompasses 43,607 acres (68.1 sq. mi) on Cape Cod. It includes ponds, woods and beachfront of the Atlantic coastal pine barrens ecoregion. The CCNS includes nearly 40 miles of seashore along the Atlantic-facing eastern shore of Cape Cod, in the towns of Provincetown, Truro, Wellfleet, Eastham, Orleans and Chatham. It is administered by the National Park Service.

Cape Cod Rail Trail

The **Cape Cod Rail Trail** is a 25.5-mile paved rail trail that passes through the towns of Yarmouth, Dennis, Harwich, Brewster, Orleans, Eastham, and Wellfleet. It connects to the 6-plus mile Old Colony Rail Trail leading to Chatham, the 2 mile Yarmouth multi-use trail, and 8 miles of trails within Nickerson State Park. Short side trips on roads lead to national seashore beaches including Coast Guard Beach at the end of the Nauset Bike Trail in Cape Cod National Seashore. In July 2020, the state awarded $181,000 for design of Phase 3 of the extension project, which will extend the trail west from Peter Horner Park in Yarmouth to Mary Dunn Road in Barnstable. Because that section of the rail line is still in use, the trail will follow a different route to the south.

Cape Cod Symphony Orchestra

The **Cape Cod Symphony**, through the leadership of Artistic Director and Conductor Jung-Ho Pak, has emerged as one of the finest community orchestras in the country. It is a constant source of enjoyment to its concert goers.

Because Cape Symphony Artistic Director & Conductor Jung-Ho Pak has worked with world-class artists like Yo-Yo Ma and James Taylor, and has conducted orchestras around the world, it's hard to imagine him in a high school rock band. He will agree the band was not very good, but it was part of his foray into music. Initially coerced into piano lessons, Jung-Ho eventually picked up the clarinet. When a generous band instructor gave him the chance to conduct, it ignited his true passion.

The season includes five Masterpiece and three Cape Pops performances, plus a New Year's Day Party and a special June event, all held in the 1,400-seat Barnstable Performing Arts Center in Hyannis. During the summer, the orchestra performs for residents and vacationers at outdoor events, including the annual Symphony at the Seashore which takes place at the Cape Cod National Seashore.

The Cape Symphony is supported by trustees and staff sponsors, supporters and volunteers.

There is no better statement than what Jung-Ho has said about the goals of the orchestra, "As artists, we have a responsibility to encourage humanity in our society. I do what I do to help make the world a better place. It's not just about presenting Beethoven and Mozart; it's about helping people connect with who they are and with each other."

If you like music you will like the Cape Cod Symphony.

John F. Kennedy Hyannis Museum

Visit the **John F. Kennedy Hyannis Museum** to learn about the legacy of President Kennedy and his deep connection to Cape Cod where he enjoyed many summers with family and friends. The Cape was the one place he could relax and feel at home, even while bearing the weight of the world. Step into the unforgettable Hyannis Port days of the 1960s when a beloved President and his family brought joy and hope to a nation. The Museum exhibits focus on his life on Cape Cod and is located at 397 Main Street, Hyannis.

Nickerson State Park

Nickerson State Park is a state-owned, public recreation area of more than 1,900 acres located in Brewster. The park's sandy soil and scrub pines surround many kettle ponds which are dependent on groundwater and precipitation. The largest of these are Cliff Pond (the largest at 0.7 miles), Flax Pond, Little Cliff Pond, and Higgins Pond. Ruth Pond, Keeler's Pond, Eel Pond, and Triangle Pond provide additional water habitats.

The land composing the park was once part of the estate of Samuel Mayo Nickerson (1830–1914), a native of the area and a Chicago liquor distiller who made a fortune as one of the founding officers of the First National Bank of Chicago. In 1890, Nickerson built Fieldstone Hall on land overlooking Cape Cod Bay a mile west of the park to be the home of his son Roland C. Nickerson, Roland's wife Addie, and their three children. Fieldstone Hall was lost to fire in 1906, and a larger mansion was built on the same site. That building subsequently became a seminary and is now a major feature of the Ocean Edge resort.

Roland Nickerson died at age 51 shortly after Fieldstone Hall burned down. His son Roland Jr. was a naval lieutenant who died in the 1918 influenza epidemic. In 1934, Addie Nickerson donated the portion of the estate on the south side of Route 6a for use as a "state forest park." It became the Commonwealth's first state park and was named in honor of her late husband and late son.

Scenic Route 6A

Massachusetts Route 6A is the state road for two sections formerly known as U.S. Route 6 (US 6) on Cape Cod. Most of Route 6A is also known as the Old King's Highway. Combining the 2 major sections (and a "silent" concurrency with US 6 through Eastham, Wellfleet, and South Truro), the highway is approximately 62 miles long.

6A began its life as a Native American Trail that evolved into a stagecoach and then into the road it is today. It became known as the King's Highway in the 1799's because so many loyalists to the King lived along the highway. Even today you can still see on some of the houses along 6A white chimneys with a black border. At one time this signed the home of a loyalist.

Driving along Route 6A in Sandwich, Barnstable and parts of Yarmouth reminds the visitor of the days when Cape Cod was much quieter and the pace of live was slower. As you drive along on this section you will pass four centuries of house architecture.

The Cape Cinema

The Cape Cinema is a movie theatre located in Dennis. It specializes in independent American and international film, simulcasts of the Metropolitan Opera and National Theatre, and live music performances.

The Cape Cinema was founded in 1930 by Edna B. Tweedy and Raymond Moore, three years after Moore founded the Cape Playhouse. The building's exterior was designed by Alfred Easton Poor and modeled after the South Congregational Church in Centerville. The auditorium is designed in the Art Deco style and includes 317 individual arm chairs of black lacquer and tangerine suede produced by the Frankl Galleries in New York. Moore and Tweedy commissioned American painter and illustrator Rockwell Kent to design a 6,400-square-foot mural for the auditorium's ceiling, featuring a representation of the heavens and constellations, and it was installed by set designer Jo Mielziner. Since 1986, the Cape Cinema has operated as an independent art house, and in 2008 it launched a live music series which has spotlighted artists such as Bon Iver, Dirty Projectors, Glen Hansard, Saint Vincent, The Paper Kites, Tift Merritt, Martha Wainwright and Pat Fee.

In 1939, the Cape Cinema was the first theatre to preview The Wizard of Oz before its Hollywood premier. The Cape Cinema is owned by the Cape Cod Center for the Arts, which includes the Cape Playhouse.

The Cape Playhouse

The **Cape Playhouse**, being named one of the 50 Best Small Stage Theatres in America, has a special place in American theatre history as the longest-running professional summer theater in the country. Referred to as the "Place Where Broadway Goes to Summer" by The New York Times, The Cape Playhouse has attracted a long litany of famous actors since its inception in 1927 including Julie Andrews, Bernadette Peters, Olympia Dukakis, Bette Davis, Henry Fonda, Betty White, Gertrude Lawrence, Gregory Peck, Humphrey Bogart, Robert Montgomery, Shirley Booth and Ginger Rogers, to name a few.

In the 1920s, founder Raymond Moore wanted to create a summer theatre close to Boston and the more affluent Cape communities. He purchased three-and-a-half acres of land fronting the Old King's Highway in Dennis and found the abandoned 19th century Nobscussett meetinghouse located in another part of Dennis. Amazingly, Moore had the large meetinghouse hauled down the road and placed on its present site.

Before air conditioning, New York was unbearable in the summer. The theatres would close, and people escaped the heat by traveling to the coastal resorts. By offering actors the prospect of paid summer work in a professional theatre away from the heat of New York City, Moore convinced the big-name stars to come perform at the new theatre.

On July 4, 1927, members of the glamorous audience watched the curtain rise on a glittering production of The Guardsman, starring Basil Rathbone and Violet Kemble Cooper – and when it rained, the roof leaked so badly that the audience put up umbrellas! Undaunted, audiences began flocking to Dennis to see the stars.

Young, unknown Bette Davis first worked as an usher before returning the following summer to act. And one promising student named Jane was given a small role in a play starring her father, Henry Fonda.

Provincetown

Provincetown /ˈprɒvɪnsˌtaʊn/ is located at the extreme tip of Cape Cod in Barnstable County. A small coastal resort town with a year-round population of 3,664 as of the 2020 US Census, Provincetown has a summer population as high as 60,000.] Often called "P-town" or "P'town", the locale is known for its beaches, harbor, artists, tourist industry, and as a popular vacation destination for the LGBT+ community.

At the time of European encounter, the area was long settled by the historic Nauset tribe, who had a settlement known as "Meeshawn." They spoke Massachusett, a Southern New England Algonquian language dialect that they shared in common with their closely related neighbors, the Wampanoag.

On 14 June 1727, after harboring ships for more than a century, the Precinct of Cape Cod was incorporated as a township. The name chosen by its inhabitants was "Herringtown", which was rejected by the Massachusetts General Court in favor of "Provincetown." The act of incorporation provided that inhabitants of Provincetown could be landholders, but not landowners. They received a quit claim to their property, but the Province retained the title. The land was to be used as it had been from the beginning of the colony — a place for the making of fish. All resources, including the trees, could be used for that purpose. In 1893 the Massachusetts General Court changed the Town's charter, giving the townspeople deeds to the properties they held, while still reserving unoccupied areas.

The population of Provincetown remained small through most of the 18th century.

In the mid-1960s, Provincetown saw population growth. The town's rural character appealed to the hippies of the era; property was relatively cheap and rents were correspondingly low, especially during the winter. Many of those who came stayed and raised families. Commercial Street, the town's equivalent to "Main Street", gained numerous cafés, leather shops, head shops – various hip small businesses blossomed and many flourished.

By the 1970s, Provincetown had a significant gay population, especially during the summer tourist season, when restaurants, bars and small shops serving the tourist trade were open. There had been a gay presence in Provincetown as early as the start of the 20th century as the artists' colony developed, along with experimental theatre. Drag queens could be seen in performance as early as the 1940s in Provincetown. In 1978 the Provincetown Business Guild (PBG) was formed to promote gay tourism. Today more than two hundred businesses belong to the PBG, and Provincetown is perhaps the best-known gay summer resort on the East Coast. The 2010 US Census revealed Provincetown to have the highest rate of same-sex couples in the country, at 163.1 per one thousand households.

Woods Hole Oceanographic Institute

At its founding in 1930, the **Woods Hole Oceanographic Institution** joined a thriving ocean science community in the village of Woods Hole, which included the Marine Biological Laboratory and the National Marine Fisheries Service. At the time, the world was only a little more than 50 years removed from the first efforts to systematically study the ocean.

The idea for WHOI dates to the early 1920s and the first of a series of conferences between Frank R. Lillie, then the MBL director, and Wickliffe Rose, then president of the Rockefeller Foundation's General Education Board. Their discussions resulted in the 1927 appointment of a National Academy of Sciences Committee on Oceanography "to consider the share of the United States of America in a world-wide program of Oceanographic Research."

The committee, chaired by Lillie, recommended that oceanographic activities on the West Coast be strengthened and that a well-equipped oceanographic institution be established on the East Coast. After considering many sites, Woods Hole was chosen for its established scientific research community, extensive library facilities, ready access both to the deep sea, to the contrasting conditions north and south of Cape Cod, a small but deep-water harbor suitable for berthing oceanographic vessels, and its proximity to several universities.

WHOI's leadership in ocean science and engineering has resulted in a long line of notable discoveries and advancements in knowledge of the ocean. These range from the distribution and role of microbes in the marine environment to development of revolutionary new tools and techniques to study the ocean to the discovery of life in the deep ocean near hydrothermal vents to a deeper understanding of the nature and impacts of hydrocarbons in the ocean.

Today, the WHOI community numbers over 1,000, including scientific and technical staff, ships' crew and officers, and a variety of scientific, service, and administrative support staff, as well as about 130 Joint Program students. All of these individuals contribute to a common goal: to help advance research and understanding of the ocean and its role in shaping and sustaining the planet. It is not a mission that WHOI takes lightly, now or at any time over the course of its history. The ocean is too important to all of us.

> "As they say on my own Cape Cod, a rising tide lifts all the boats."
>
> Author: John F. Kennedy

Cape Cod Indigenous People
The Wampanoag Tribe

Cape Cod was occupied for more than ten thousand years by indigenous peoples. The historic Algonquian speaking Wampanoag were the native people encountered by the English colonists here and in the area of the Massachusetts Bay Colony in the seventeenth century. The Wampanoag also controlled considerable coastal area. These two cultures would interact, shaping each other for decades.

The **Wampanoag** /ˈwɑːmpənɔːg/, also rendered **Wôpanâak**, are a Native American people. They were a loose confederation of several tribes in the 17th century, but today Wampanoag people encompass five officially recognized tribes. The Mashpee Wampanoag Tribe and the Wampanoag Tribe of Gay Head in Massachusetts are federally recognized, and the Chappaquiddick, Herring Pond, Assawompsett-Nemasket Band of Wampanoags, and Pocasset Wampanoag Tribe (Pokonoket) are recognized by the Commonwealth of Massachusetts. They lived in southeastern Massachusetts and Rhode Island in the beginning of the 17th century, at the time of first contact with the English colonists, their population numbered in the thousands; 3,000 Wampanoag lived on Martha's Vineyard alone.

From 1615 to 1619, the Wampanoag suffered an epidemic, long suspected to be smallpox. It caused a high fatality rate and decimated the Wampanoag population. More than 50 years later, King Philip's War (1675–1676) of the Narragansett and their allies against the colonists and their Native American allies resulted in the death of 40 percent of the surviving tribe. Many male Wampanoag were sold into slavery in Bermuda or the West Indies, and some women and children were enslaved by colonists in New England.

In 1620, the Pilgrims arrived in Plymouth, and Tisquantum and other Wampanoag taught them how to cultivate the varieties of corn, squash, and beans (the Three Sisters) that flourished in New England, as well as how to catch and process fish and collect seafood. They enabled the Pilgrims to survive their first winters, and Squanto lived with them and acted as a middleman between them and Massasoit, the Wampanoag sachem.

The tribe disappeared from historical records after the late 18th century, although its people and descendants persisted. Survivors continued to live in their traditional areas and maintained many aspects of their culture, while absorbing other peoples by marriage and adapting to changing economic and cultural needs in the larger society.

The Wampanoag people were semi-sedentary, with seasonal movements between sites in southern New England. The men often traveled far north and south along the Eastern seaboard for seasonal fishing expeditions, and sometimes stayed in those distant locations for weeks and months at a time. The women cultivated varieties of the "three sisters" (maize, climbing beans, and squash) as the staples of their diet, supplemented by fish and game caught by the men. Each community had authority over a well-defined territory from which the people derived their livelihood through a seasonal round of fishing, planting, harvesting, and hunting. Southern New England was populated by various tribes, so hunting grounds had strictly defined boundaries.

The Wampanoag had a matrilineal system, like many indigenous peoples of the Northeastern Woodlands, in which women controlled property, and hereditary status was passed through the maternal line. They were also matrifocal; when a young couple married, they lived with the woman's family. Women elders could approve selection of chiefs or sachems. Men acted in most of the political roles for relations with other bands and tribes, as well as warfare. Women passed plots of land to their female descendants, regardless of their marital status.

The Wampanoag were organized into a confederation in which a head sachem presided over a number of other sachems. The colonists often referred to him as "king," but the position of a sachem differed in many ways from a king. They were selected by women elders and were bound to consult their own councilors within their tribe, as well as any of the "petty sachems" in the region. They were also responsible for arranging trade privileges, as well as protecting their allies in exchange for material tribute. Both women and men could hold the position of sachem, and women were sometimes chosen over close male relatives.

Pre-marital sexual experimentation was accepted, although the Wampanoag expected fidelity within unions after marriage. Roger Williams (1603–1683) said that "single fornication they count no sin, but after Marriage... they count it heinous for either of them to be false." Polygamy was practiced among the Wampanoag, although monogamy was the norm. Some elite men could take several wives for political or social reasons, and multiple wives were a symbol of wealth. Women were the producers and distributors of corn and other food products. Marriage and conjugal unions were not as important as ties of clan and kinship.

The rapid decline of Wampanoag speakers began after the American Revolution. Since 1993, some Wampanoag have been working on a language revival.

The Wôpanâak (Wampanoag) Language Reclamation Project is a collaboration of several tribes and bands led by Jessie Little Doe Baird. They have taught some children, who have become the first speakers of Wôpanâak in more than 100 years. The project is training teachers to reach more children and to develop a curriculum for a Wôpanâak-based school. Baird has developed a 10,000-word Wôpanâak-English dictionary by consulting archival Wôpanâak documents and using linguistic methods to reconstruct unattested words. She has also produced a grammar, collections of stories, and other books. Mashpee High School began a course in 2018 teaching the language.

The Mashpee Wampanoag Tribe, also known as the People of the First Light, has inhabited present day Massachusetts and Eastern Rhode Island for more than 12,000 years. After an arduous process lasting more than three decades, the Mashpee Wampanoag were re-acknowledged as a federally recognized tribe in 2007. In 2015, the federal government declared 150 acres of land in Mashpee and 170 acres of land in Taunton as the Tribe's initial reservation, on which the Tribe can exercise its full tribal sovereignty rights. The Mashpee tribe currently has approximately 2,600 enrolled citizens.

For more detail information about the Tribe visit their museum in Mashpee.

A statue of Katherine Lee Bates, who wrote the lyrics to *America the Beautful*, is located on the grounds of the Falmouth Memorial Library.

Women of Cape Cod

Unfortunately, many women who have had a major impact Cape Cod's past were not given the recognition that they deserved. Here are some of the women who have been recognized.

Susanna White The mother who gave birth to Peregrine White, the first child born on board the Mayflower after the ship anchored off Cape Cod.

Katharine Lee Bates (August 12, 1859 – March 28, 1929) was an American professor and author, chiefly remembered for her anthem "America the Beautiful," but also for her many books and articles on social reform, on which she was a noted speaker.

She was born in Falmouth, Massachusetts, to the town's Congregational minister William Bates and Cornelia Frances Lee. Bates died in Wellesley, Massachusetts, She is buried in Oak Grove Cemetery at Falmouth. Most of her papers are housed at the Wellesley College Archives.

Bates enjoyed close links with Wellesley College where she had graduated with a B.A., and later became a professor of English literature, helping to launch American literature as an academic specialty, and writing one of the first-ever college textbooks on it. She never married, possibly because she would have lost tenure if she had. Throughout her long career at Wellesley, she shared a house with her close friend and companion Katharine Coman. Some scholars have assumed that this was a lesbian relationship, considering some exchanges of letters sufficient proof, others believe their relationship may have been a platonic "Boston marriage" in the contemporary phrase.

The first draft of "America the Beautiful" was hastily jotted down in a notebook during the summer of 1893, which Bates spent teaching English at Colorado College in Colorado Springs, Colorado. Later she remembered:

"One day some of the other teachers and I decided to go on a trip to 14,000-foot Pikes Peak. We hired a prairie wagon. Near the top we had to leave the wagon and go the rest of the way on mules. I was very tired. But when I saw the view, I felt great joy. All the wonder of America seemed displayed there, with the sea-like expanse."

Adele R. Heller Passionate supporter of the arts, Adele R. Heller (1922-1997) revived the historic Provincetown Playhouse as owner and producing director, and continued to memorialize the plays of Eugene O'Neill, which first debuted onstage in Provincetown. She was the prolific author of 1915, the Cultural Moment, an academic study of this pivotal year in American theatrical history and the era's progressive movements, which is still widely referenced today. Before leaving New York to settle for good on Cape Cod, Heller worked for Adam Clayton Powell, America's first African American Congressman, and helped found our nation's Head Start program. An accomplished artist herself, Heller was an award-winning haiku poet and concert pianist who championed musical and artistic life in Provincetown, where she spent every summer until finally relocating in 1980.

Rosemary Rapp An artist and avid collector herself of early American and 19th century artwork, Rosemary Rapp founded the non-profit Cahoon Museum of American Art in Cotuit in 1984. She followed her fervent desire to preserve the story, artwork and historic structure that served as the home and studio of celebrated Cape Cod artists Ralph Cahoon (1910-1982) and Martha Cahoon (1905-1999), who worked side by side as decorative furniture painters and folk artists. In true visionary fashion, Rapp undertook a major museum renovation and remodel to increase accessibility and double exhibition space, which was completed and celebrated in 2016. Today's museum collection includes American art representing every medium, including fine art, contemporary and three-dimensional art, works on paper, and furniture dating from the 18th century to the present.

Rachel Carson An outdoor sculpture depicting the biologist, conservationist, and author, Rachel Carson, was installed in Waterfront Park in Woods Hole on July 14, 2013. It was to mark the 50th anniversary of the publishing of Rachel Carson's book *Silent Springs*, an environmental science book. The book was published on September 27, 1962, documenting the adverse environmental effects caused by the indiscriminate use of pesticides. Carson accused the chemical industry of spreading disinformation, and public officials of accepting the industry's marketing claims unquestioningly. The inscription on a plaque at the site of the sculptor reads:

"I had my first prolonged contact with the sea at Woods Hole. Never tired of watching the tidal currents pouring through the hole – that wonderful place of whirlpools and eddies and swiftly racing waters."

Portuguese Matriarchs The installation, "They Also Faced the Sea," was originally printed over a decade ago to honor Provincetown's fishing and Portuguese heritage Now it is five photographs of Portuguese women that have been installed on Fisherman's wharf in Provincetown. It honors the women who stayed home while their husbands were at sea.

Anna Howard Shaw Reverend, physician, and suffragist? There is nothing a woman cannot do, and Anna Howard Shaw (1847-1919) of Osterville was living proof. After feeling called to ministry and paying heavily for being the only woman in her class, she was the second woman to graduate from Boston University School of Theology and one of the first to be ordained by the Methodist Protestant Church. During her ministry (one was in East Dennis), she earned her medical degree from Boston University. Eventually her preaching became worldwide and swelled to include issues of social justice and women's rights. Susan B. Anthony solicited Shaw to be her protégé, and a prime force behind the adoption of the 19th amendment. Shaw served as president of the National American Woman Suffrage Association for over a decade and was on the campaign trail constantly with company that included Ralph Waldo Emerson, Louisa May Alcott, Frederick Douglas, and US presidents. She died just before the suffrage amendment was ratified.

She is known for this quote: "I am happy in having known and loved the Cape as it was, and in having gathered there a store of delightful memories. In later strenuous years, it rested me merely to think of the place."

Margaret Moseley Community peace and civil rights activist Margaret Moseley (1901-1997) graduated from Dedham High in 1919 but was unable to pursue a career in nursing due to racial discrimination. A true humanitarian, she viewed her personal suffering as insight for understanding the same suffering of larger numbers of people who did not have the self-belief to speak out and rose to activism. Years later, after moving to the Cape in 1961, she helped establish local chapters of the National Association for the Advancement of Colored People and talked with the Sunday school children at the Unitarian Church of Barnstable about meeting Martin Luther King in 1958. Moseley's unwavering fight against prejudice and injustice and devotion to her local community led her to identify one of Cape Cod's greatest needs as nondiscrimination and non-segregation in housing. She responded by founding the first Fair Housing Committee.

Alice Foley She played a huge role in taking care of the Provincetown community and was a trailblazer in the fight against AIDS. Not only was she the town nurse who oversaw the care of Provincetown's elderly and low-income residents, she served as executive director of the AIDS Support Group — a group which she founded from the back seat of her car in the mid-1980s.

Molly Benjamin She was a captain of her own boat, played an instrumental role in bringing clam farming to Provincetown, and according to a 1996 article from The New York Times, Yankee Magazine named her "one of the 60 people who make New England, New England."

> "I grew up on Cape Cod. We didn't live right on the water, but I could walk to it and did every day."
>
> Author: Andrea Barrett

So, You Think You Know Cape Cod?

Trivia Questions

1. Where do you go if you want to see the entire Cape Cod on a clear day?
2. There is only one town on Cape Cod that does not have an English or Native American name?
3. What town on Cape Cod is known as the "sea captains' town?"
4. Where was the home of shipbuilding on Cape Cod during the golden era of shipbuilding?
5. How long is the longest round-trip hike in the National Seashore Park?
6. What draws the great white shark into the waters off Cape Cod?
7. What is the longest beach on Cape Cod?
8. What is the best beach for surfing on Cape Cod?
9. Where do the Pilgrims and the Native Americans first meet?
10. What is the tribe of the Native Americans that first greeted the Pilgrims on First Encounter Bach?
11. The National Seashore has how many miles of shoreline?
12. What gives the Wellfleet oysters their salty, sweet flavor?
13. What is Cape Cod's favorite flower
14. Where is there a village of dune shacks?
15. What are the ingredients of a traditional Cape Codder cocktail?
16. What does "Doug the Quahog" do every first day of summer?
17. When was Cape Cod separated from the mainland?
18. Why is the distance of the Falmouth Road Race seven miles?
19. When was the Wampanoag tribe federally recognized?
20. What is the most attended museum on Cape Cod?
21. What is the best kid-friendly beach trail on Cape Cod?
22. With more than 7,600 acres of protected dunes, salt, and fresh-water marshes and a decommissioned lighthouse, the gorgeous Monomoy National Wildlife Refuge will make you feel like a trailblazer. What else is there that is very important?

23. What is the Hidden Hollow?
24. Where were the Pilgrims going when they spotted Cape Cod?
25. In May of 1602, Bartholomew Gosnold set foot on Cape Cod as the first know European. What name did he initially give to the land?
26. Are there bears on Cape Cod?
27. There are seven known great mammals on Cape Cod. Five of them are – coyotes, foxes, deer, turkeys, and fishers. Do you know the other two?
28. If you are asked, "where is the best spot for birdwatching on Cape Cod? Your answer should be....?
29. Where does the Cape Cod Central Railroad begin and end?
30. What was the Sagamore Hill Military Reservation located in the Scusset Beach State Reservation?
31. How many books were discovered in the home of Edward Gorey after he died?
32. Are there any ruined structures on Great Island?
33. The Lowell Holly Reservation spans 135 acres between two towns. What are they?
34. The Town of Hyannis and the District of Wianno are named after tribal chiefs from what tribe?
35. During the King Phillips War (1675-1676), who did the Nauset Tribe fight for and against?
36. There are more lighthouses on Cape Cod than in ....?
37. The land on the southern tip of West Yarmouth's Great Island, just east of the entrance to Hyannis Harbor, is named Point Gammon. What is the origin of the name Gammon?
38. What was the first lighthouse built on Cape Cod?
39. Where are the Dune Shacks located?
40. Kettle Ponds are scattered throughout the outer Cape. What are they?
41. If you are in Centerville and want penny candy, where do you go?
42. Who was the Bourne high school graduate who played football at the University of Michigan and later played for the NFL Broncos and Patriots?

So, You Think You Know Cape Cod?

43. Where did the artist Edward Hopper have a summer home?
44. What town of the Cape was once named one of the happiest towns in America?
45. What town is located on both sides of the Cape Cod Canal?
46. If you are watching fireworks over Oyster Pond, where are you?
47. What lies directly south of Chatham along the coast?
48. What was the purpose of the Truro Air Force base?
49. Who founded the Cape Cod Museum for Children?
50. If you are in Truro and want to visit a winery, where do you go?
51. The clock on Wellfleet's First Congregational Church is the only town clock in the world that strikes the time in what medium?
52. Where did the name Fort Hill originate?
53. You are standing on the main thoroughfare of a town on Cape Cod, named "Commercial Street" where are you?
54. In what town can you find the largest rubber duck collection in the world?
55. You are standing in front of the John F. Kennedy Museum; what street are you on, and what town are you in?
56. If you are standing in front of Hot Diggity (1 Central Square), where are you?
57. What is the oldest town on Cape Cod?
58. What is known as the "Art Gallery Town?"
59. If you leave the Irish Pub & Restaurant and go to Bear in Boots Gastropub, where are you?
60. If you are on Cahoon Hollow Beach watching the sunrise, where are you?
61. If you are standing on Uncle Tim's Bridge overlooking Duck Creek, where are you?
62. If you are attending Fantasia Week, where are you?
63. How can you get to see some of the private gardens on Cape Cod?
64. What theater on Cape Cod hosted the world premiere of the movie "The Wizard of Oz?"

65. Barnstable County has more of what than any other county in America?
66. Amrita Island lies in the Cataumet section of Bourne. What is the origin of the name?
67. How many prisoners can the old wooden Barnstable Jail hold?
68. The Dutch-style windmill built of wood was first erected near the town line of Sandwich and Barnstable on the north side of Cape Cod, making it one of the oldest windmills in the country. Where is it today?
69. If you are at the Wellfleet Drive-In and your 1950 speaker does not work, what do you do to get sound?
70. If you are looking for the largest flea market on Cape Cod, where would you go?
71. Where can you find the 80-year-old ruins of the Barnstable Brick Co.?
72. If you want to see the Lobster Trap Christmas Tree, where should you go?
73. The Days' Cottages are painted white with green trim, so how are they distinguished?
74. When were the Days' Cottages built?
75. The Poppy Spit separates two bodies of water; what are they?
76. If you see silvery-hued fish swimming in the shallow water, what beach are you on?
77. How many villages are in Falmouth?
78. Where is Dowses Beach?
79. The Brewster Flats are the largest in North America. How many acres at low tide make up the Flats?
80. What are the towns that share Pleasant Bay?
81. What became of "The Lost Island" of Wellfleet, Billingsgate, that was located 2.5 miles off the shore of Wellfleet.?
82. Why is Fort Hill's history important to the history of Cape Cod?

Trivia Answers

1. Scargo Tower in Dennis
2. Orleans
3. Brewster
4. Dennis
5. Nine miles.
6. Seal poop.
7. Sandy Beach is six miles long.
8. White Crest Beach in Wellfleet (sometimes called four-mile or surfer's beach) is known for its great longboard waves.
9. First Encounter Beach in Eastham
10. They were members of the Nauset tribe of the Wampanoag Nation.
11. 40 miles
12. They are farmed in protected flats of cold, fast-moving, pristine waters.
13. Hydrangea
14. Cape Cod National Seashore Park
15. Vodka, cranberry juice, and a wedge of lime are considered a traditional Cape Codder cocktail.
16. He predicts the number of days the Cape will enjoy sunshine.
17. In 1914, when the Cape Canal construction was completed.
18. The reason for the unusual distance is that the man who thought the race up (Tommy Leonard) was a bartender who wanted a race along the coast from one bar (The Cap'n Kidd in Woods Hole) to another (The Brothers Four in Falmouth Heights, later the British Beer Company).
19. May 2007
20. The Provincetown Art Association and Museum
21. The Fort Hill Trail in Eastham offers beautiful wildflowers and flat terrain great for small children.
22. North and South Monomoy is a nesting habitat for hundreds of species of migratory seabirds.

23. It is a two-acre children's play area in the Heritage Garden in Sandwich.
24. Virginia
25. Shoal Hope
26. No, but there was one in 2012, and he was removed to the mainland.
27. Bats and racoons
28. Wellfleet Bay Wildlife Sanctuary encompasses salt marshes, sandy barrier beaches, and pine woodlands and is home to threatened shorebirds, sea turtles, diamondback terrapins, and horseshoe crabs. Birdwatchers have spotted more than 300 species in the various ecosystems of the wildlife sanctuary.
29. It runs between Hyannis and Buzzards Bay.
30. A World War II Coastal Military Reservation, first established in 1941 in Barnstable County and abandoned in 1945. It was part of the defense of Boston Harbor.
31. 25,000
32. Yes, in Great Beach Hill, there is a ruined camp made of cinder blocks and built into the side of the hill.
33. Sandwich and Mashpee
34. Nauset Native American Chiefs
35. The Nauset tribe fought with the Pilgrims against the Wampanoag Tribe.
36. The world.
37. "Gammon" comes from an old term that means "to deceive or fool," and Point Gammon is aptly named for the treacherous waters that deceived sailors and resulted in lost ships and lives.
38. Highland Light in Truro was built in 1797.
39. The Dune Shacks are located in Peaked Hill Bars Historic District, which is in the Cape Cod National Seashore, and covers an area of approximately 1,900 acres of beautiful and eroding dunes.
40. A kettle is a depression/hole in an outwash plain formed by retreating glaciers or draining floodwaters. The kettles are formed due to blocks of dead ice left behind by retreating glaciers, which become surrounded by sediment deposited by meltwater streams with increased friction. The ice becomes

buried in the sediment, and when the ice melts, a depression is left called a kettle hole, creating a dimpled appearance on the outwash. Ponds often fill these kettles; these are called kettle hole ponds.

41. The 1856 Country Store
42. Robert Lewis "Bob" Perryman, Jr
43. Truro
44. Barnstable
45. Bourne
46. In Chatham
47. Monomoy Natural Wildlife Refuge
48. The Truro Air Force Base was built during the height of the Cold War to detect, identify, intercept, and destroy hostile aircraft. The construction of the base was a direct response to President Truman's announcement that the Soviet Union had detonated an atomic bomb.
49. A group of moms
50. Truro Vineyards
51. In ship's bells.
52. It looked out over Nauset Harbor.
53. Provincetown.
54. Chatham – Ducks in the Window Gift Shop
55. Main Street, Hyannis Village, Barnstable
56. Mashpee Commons
57. Sandwich
58. Wellfleet
59. Falmouth Center on Main Street
60. Wellfleet
61. Wellfleet
62. Provincetown
63. Attend the Hydrangea Festival, starting the first week of July.
64. The Cape Cinema in Dennis.
65. Lighthouses
66. The word Amrita is from Sanskrit Jainism and means immortality.
67. Six

68. The Farris Windmill was dismantled in 1935 and shipped more than 800 miles to Dearborn, Michigan, to become a part of Greenfield Village, Henry Ford's museum.
69. Turn on your car radio and tune into the Drive-in's radio station 98.5 FM.
70. Wellfleet Flea Market 51 US-6, Wellfleet, MA
71. Access can be gained by parking where the railroad tracks cross 6A just east of Barnstable Village and walking east next to the tracks. Note there is a lot of overgrowth; look closely.
72. Provincetown
73. Each has a different name.
74. Early 1930s
75. Nantucket Sound and Popponesset Bay
76. Old Silver Beach in Falmouth
77. Eight
78. Osterville Village, Barnstable
79. 12,000 acres
80. Chatham, Orleans, Brewster, Harwich
81. The water rose over the island, and by the early 1940s it began to be known as the Billingsgate Shoal.
82. As a high point it offered a defensive position against any incursion by Dutch from New Amsterdam.

Photos

Questions and Answers

So, You Think You Know Cape Cod?

This town on Cape Cod is famous for its swimming holes. What town?

What is the name of this trail?

Answers - page 164

So, You Think You Know Cape Cod?

Who is depicted in this photo taken in Eastham?

What is this?

Answers - page 164

So, You Think You Know Cape Cod?

What is this building?

What is this building?

Answers - page 164

So, You Think You Know Cape Cod?

What are these towers and where were they?

Who is depicted in this statue?

Answers - page 164

So, You Think You Know Cape Cod?

Where is this buoy tree located and what is it significance?

What is this?

Answers - page 164

So, You Think You Know Cape Cod?

What is the name of this field and where is it located?

What is this and where is it located?

Answers - page 164

So, You Think You Know Cape Cod?

This is the entrance to what club?

What is this and where is it located?

Answers - page 164

So, You Think You Know Cape Cod?

What is the name of the bridge in the foreground and the bridge in the background?

What is this?

Answers - page 164

So, You Think You Know Cape Cod?

It is the oldest golf course on the Cape. What is its name and location?

What is this?

Answers - page 165

So, You Think You Know Cape Cod?

Where is this jetty located?

This football field lies along the Cape Cod Canal. Whose field is it?

Answers - page 165

So, You Think You Know Cape Cod?

Where is this windmill located?

Who is depicted in this statue and where is it?

Answers - page 165

So, You Think You Know Cape Cod?

What is the name of this statue?

Can you identify this building?

Answers - page 165

So, You Think You Know Cape Cod?

Photo Answers

Page 152, top: Harwich is famous for its swimming holes.

Page 152, bottom: This is a railroad trail that goes from Sandwich to Wellfleet.

Page 153, top: Buffalo soldiers who were the forerunners of the park rangers. They were African American soldiers who fought in the civil war.

Page 153, bottom photo: This is a motor propeller from a Coast Guard rescue boat. It saved 32 men from the ship the Pendleton that sunk off Chatham during a storm.

Page 154, top: The Gray Gables train depot was built for the personal use of President Grover Cleveland. The depot is located in the Gray Gables Village of Bourne.

Page 154, bottom: Falmouth Town Hall

Page 155, top: Marconi wireless sending towers are located in Wellfleet.

Page 155, bottom: This statue on the green in Hyannis, by Cape Cod sculptor David Lewis, commemorates Chief Sachem Iyanough who befriended early settlers.

Page 156, top: The Buoy Tree in Eastham represents the original built and lit up each year by town resident James Filliman. Friends and family build this tree each year as a tribute to Jimmy, who died in 2018, and as a testament to Eastham's true community spirit.

Page 156, bottom: America's first rotary and it is in South Yarmouth.

Page 157, top: Veteran's Field in Chatham

Page 157, bottom: It is a crypt and is located in Pine Grove Cemetery in Truro

Page 158, top: Oyster Harbors Club

Page 158, bottom: Wampanoag - Native American dwelling

Page 159, top: Railroad Bridge and the Bourne Bridge

Page 159, bottom: The Aids Memorial that is located in Provincetown

Page 160, top: Highland Links Golf Course North Truro

Page 160, bottom: The inclined elevator system that ferries visitors up an 85-ft slope to the top of High Pole Hill—and the Pilgrim Monument—from the streets of downtown Provincetown.

Page 161, top: Scusset State Park in Sagamore Beach

Page 161, bottom: Massachusetts Maritime Academy

Page 162, top: The windmill is on the grounds of the Aptucxet Museum Complex in Bourne.

Page 162, bottom: The statue is of Rachel Carson, author of *Silent Spring*, and it is located in Wood Hole.

Page 163, top: The Head of the Cod and Tail of the Fish statue is located in the Cahoon Museum of American Art in Cotuit, a village in the Town of Barnstable. This dramatic swimming fish sculpture celebrates the importance of the Atlantic Codfish to the history, economy, and ecology of Cape Cod and New England.

Page 163, bottom: West Parish of Barnstable, United Church of Christ.